The
Roman Siege of
Jerusalem

The
Roman Siege of
Jerusalem by Rupert Furneaux

Hart-Davis MacGibbon
London

Granada Publishing Limited
First published in Great Britain by Rupert Hart-Davis Ltd
3 Upper James Street London W1R 4BP

ISBN 0 246 10520 8
Printed in Great Britain by
Northumberland Press Ltd,
Gateshead

Acknowledgements

The author gratefully acknowledges the help given him by Professor M. Avi-Yonah, of the Hebrew University, Jerusalem, who conducted him through the Ancient City and elsewhere.

Unless otherwise credited, quotations from Josephus's works reprinted by permission of Loeb Classical Library, Harvard University Press and Heinemann Educational Books Ltd, London.

Quotations from *The Messiah Jesus and John the Baptist* by R. Eisler reprinted by permission of Dial Press, New York, and Methuen & Co. Ltd, London.

Quotations from *Sulpicius Severus and Titus' Council of War* by H. W. Montefiore, *Historia XI*.

Contents

List of Illustrations

List of Tables
and Maps

PART I
Resistance,
A.D. 6-66

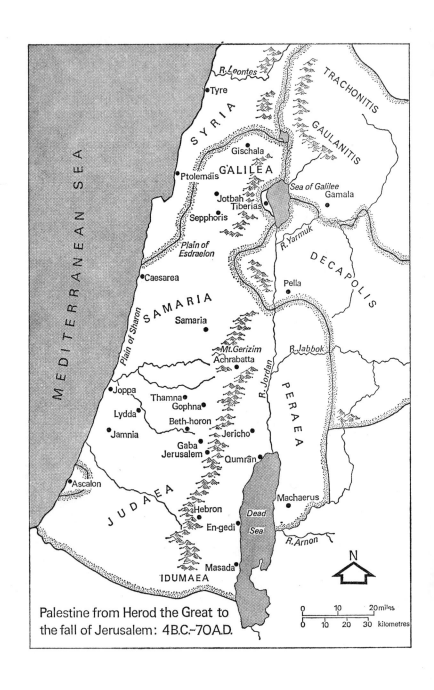

Palestine from Herod the Great to
the fall of Jerusalem: 4B.C.–70A.D.

One

The Ancient
Quisling

Twice daily for sixty years the Jews had sacrificed, in the Temple at Jerusalem, two lambs and a bull on behalf of the Emperor and the Roman people. The offering symbolized Jewish loyalty and subservience to Imperial Rome.

In the summer of A.D. 66, supported by revolutionaries and encouraged by the lesser priests, the Captain of the Temple, a daring youth named Eleazar, stopped the sacrifice—an act of rebellion.

Eleazar besieged the Roman garrison in the Antonia fortress which overlooked the Temple. Menahem, the Zealot leader, marched his men to the Dead Sea, where by a stratagem they captured the rock fortress of Masada. Killing the Roman garrison, they equipped themselves from the extensive armoury. Menahem returned in triumph to Jerusalem. He was acclaimed the Messiah-King, gaining immense prestige from his ancestry. He was the son of Judas of Galilee, who, at the time of the Census of Jewish Citizens by Quirinius in A.D. 6, had founded the sect, or politico-religious party, of the Zealots.

These extreme nationalists inspired—and sixty years later became the soul and body of—the Great Revolt of the Jews, dying in the last defence. Their choice of mass suicide on the hilltop of Masada in preference to Roman servitude has inspired the Israelis of today. Modern archaeological discoveries at their fortress have intrigued the world. Our consequent better understanding of the Zealots has redressed the calumnies of Flavius Josephus, the eyewitness historian who called these fierce resistance fighters 'criminals' and 'bandits'. To a man of his class and prejudices, they were the most dangerous of fanatics—revolutionaries and disturbers of the established order.

Josephus, too, has suffered from misunderstanding and misrepresentation, for which he has largely himself to blame. Apart from a few other meagre references, his extensive history is our only remaining source of information about the great Jewish revolt which culminated in the siege and destruction of Jerusalem, an event of momentous and immeasurable consequences.

Because Josephus was biased, his motives need analysing before his narrative can be interpreted. He was a man of complex character—and peculiar motivations.

Joseph ben Mattathias, to give him his Jewish name, was born in Jerusalem in A.D. 37 or 38, the son of a priestly father who belonged to one of the chief families of the priesthood. His mother claimed descent from the Jewish Maccabean Kings of the ancient Hasmonaean family. Josephus, as it is convenient to call him, became a priest like his father, although he was not a member of the Sadducees, the close-knit group of noble families who monopolized the office of High Priest, and who, during the period of Roman rule, controlled Jewish affairs.

Josephus tells us that as a precocious child he was consulted at the age of fourteen by the scribes on the interpretation of difficult points of Jewish Law. He continued his education until the age of nineteen, studying under masters of the major Jewish religious sects—Sadducees, Pharisees, and Essenes. He spent three years in the wilderness with an ascetic named Bannus before finally adopting the discipline of the Pharisees.

We hear next of Josephus when, aged twenty-six in the year 64, he led a deputation to Rome on behalf of certain imprisoned Jewish priests, whose release he secured through the intervention of the Empress Poppaea, the wife of Nero. He returned to Jerusalem, where he found his countrymen bent on revolt. (Of the ambiguous part Josephus played in the ensuing war we shall learn in due course.) He was given, or took, command of Jewish forces in Galilee. In time he surrendered and then defected to the Romans, whom he accompanied for the remainder of the campaign as official historian.

Josephus wrote from the Roman point of view, entitling his history *Concerning the Jewish War*, a work that appeared in several editions. The first was probably a short record, which he may have called *On the Capture of Jerusalem*, written in his own language, Aramaic, and intended as a warning to the peoples of the Middle East of the futility and folly of war against Rome. This edition disappeared without trace. In A.D. 71 he published a further short account in the Greek language, to synchronize with the Triumph in Rome of the victorious Emperor Vespasian and his son Titus. Josephus expanded the work with the help of scholarly assistants—between the years A.D. 75 and 79—into the full history of the war. For this writing he was granted access to the Roman Archives, including the use of their official war commentaries. His history was given the imperial *imprimatur*. The modern editor of the works of Josephus, H. St J. Thackeray, has remarked that rarely could an ancient author have enjoyed such a combination of circumstances for presenting a veracious picture. (The controversial Slavonic manuscripts of a short version are discussed in the Appendix.)

Josephus was obviously not an impartial historian. Accorded Roman citizenship, a pension, and the use of a royal palace, he flattered his benefactors, the Emperor Vespasian and his son Titus, and adopted their family name Flavius. His history had an apologetic purpose: to shift the blame for the war from his people, who, he claimed, had been led astray by sophists and visionaries. They had been beguiled, he said, by an 'ambiguous oracle', or prediction, in their holy scriptures, which foretold that a man from Judaea was destined to rule the world.

Josephus did not wholly reject the visionary hopes of his people. Like most orthodox Jews, he believed in that divine providence which had buoyed up Jewish tenacity through long years of adversity. He rejected, however, the popular belief that God would send his mighty champion, the Messiah, at the head of twelve legions of angels to free the Jews from the bondage of pagan foreigners. He distrusted religious zeal, did not believe in miracles, and, as an educated and travelled man, felt that the small Jewish nation was incapable of challenging successfully the might of Imperial Rome.

Possibly resentful of the Zealots' ardour (in which he himself was woefully lacking), to square his conscience, and to answer his critics, Josephus indulged in much tortuous self-examination and many apologies. Some modern historians have called him an ancient Quisling. Many Jews have considered Josephus a traitor. In his various books he portrays himself as a strange mixture of renegade and patriot. He takes pains to explain his role in the war, evidently finding the necessity for explanation highly embarrassing. To some readers he seems an unscrupulous opportunist, rendered even more distasteful by his hypocritical protestations of the highest motives. Yet in his later works he appears to be a fervent believer in his religion, refusing only to accept Jewish nationalist pretensions and philosophical exclusiveness. Indeed his prudence was not without wisdom, for the war ended in the catastrophe he feared and which, if his story can be accepted, he risked his life to avert.

Whatever his failings, it is to Josephus that we owe our knowledge of a period of revolutionary change when the common people of a nation rose in revolt against the complacency of an established order which failed to understand their visionary hopes.

Following the publication of *Concerning the Jewish War*, and again later in his life, which lasted to the beginning of the second century, Josephus devoted his energies to writing the full history of his nation in the *Antiquities of the Jews*. He wrote, also, two minor works: his own *Life*, in which he challenged the accusations of a rival historian, and *Contra Apion*, a defence of Judaism. The Roman historian Tacitus is the only other writer who supplies information about the revolt of the Jews, but only up to the start of the siege of Jerusalem. One important episode is told by a later historian, who may have drawn upon the lost portion of Tacitus's work.

Another source of information cannot be ignored, for it supplies some surprising clues to the attitude of the Jews and the progress of the spirit of revolt, the very existence of which it is at pains to disguise. The historical value of the New Testament books will be discussed in connection with the episode when, during the Procuratorship of Pontius Pilate, a Jewish Messiah-King was tried and executed for the crime, in a Roman Province, of setting himself up as a usurper—a rival to Caesar. Jesus, as we shall learn, was not the only Messianic claimant, the first of whom made his bid for recognition in A.D. 6.

Two

The Messiah
Judas of Galilee

Violent Jewish resistance to the occupation of their land by foreigners, which had smouldered for thirty years during the reign of the hated Herod, burst into flame on the Roman annexation of Judaea in A.D. 6. For the assessment of tribute, Quirinius, the Imperial Legate of Syria, ordered a census—an enrolment of the population bound to make the Jews conscious of their subservience to a foreign, heathen Emperor. Prior to that date they had enjoyed some semblance of national independence under the rule of Herod the Great, who had seized power under the Romans. But Herod had married Mariamne, a Jewish princess, to establish his authority beyond a doubt. On the death of Herod in 4 B.C. the Emperor Augustus had divided Herod's dominions among his sons. Archelaus was appointed Ethnarch of Judaea, including Samaria and Idumaea. Philip was made Tetrarch of the North-eastern Province. Antipas was appointed Tetrarch of Galilee and Peraea, a position he held for thirty-three years. Archelaus's rule of Judaea ended in anarchy and, after ten years and on the complaint of his subjects, he was deposed and banished to Gaul.

The tranquillity of Palestine, which provided the strategic land-link between the Imperial provinces of Syria and Egypt and formed a barrier against the Parthian Empire to the east, was of vital concern to the Romans. They attempted to gain their subjects' passive co-operation or submission by granting complete religious freedom. The Jews were permitted to offer daily sacrifice *for* rather than *to* the Imperial Cult, an unusual dispensation for a subject people. They were also exempted from military service, another peculiar concession, and were allowed to run their own internal affairs. To this Roman attitude of self-interested good-will the various groups of Jews reacted differently, according sometimes to the depth of their religious feelings, sometimes to self-interest.

The priestly aristocrats, the small but powerful Sadducee party, were prepared to co-exist with the Romans, whose rule they may have preferred to the dangerous alternative of mob law. The Pharisees, another small party whose teachings were accepted by the majority of the population, adopted a policy of passive resistance. So, possibly, did the Essenes. The Essenes are believed to have lived in monastic seclusion, remote from mundane affairs, although this view has been challenged since the discovery of the Dead Sea Scrolls.

The belligerent owners of the Scrolls found at Qumran, if they were Essenes, were either less pacific than has long been accepted, or may have been Zealots, one of several extremist groups which heroically opposed the Roman occupation.

Josephus's imputation of patriotic resistance to the Zealots alone, and his assertion that Zealotism was a new growth, have been challenged by Professor W. R. Farmer (in *Maccabees, Zealots and Josephus*) and other modern historians, who claim that Josephus emphasized the importance of these 'bandits' to the exclusion of the ancient Jewish tradition of national resistance to foreign rule, inherited from the heroic Maccabees.

The Maccabees had opposed foreign rule between 166 and 134 B.C. Judas Maccabaeus, 'the Hammer' (as he was called), defeated the Syrian king, Antiochus Epiphanes, and restored the ancient forms of worship. Under his successors and their 'zealous' supporters, the Jews secured a semblance of political freedom. This lasted until 63 B.C., when the Romans intervened in the affairs of the Middle East.

Professor Farmer claims that Josephus ignored the tradition of national resistance to foreign rule inherited from the Maccabees because he preferred not to couple their heroic name with the, in his opinion, criminal leaders who had brought disaster upon the Jewish nation. Nor did it suit Josephus's purpose to imply that the Jews of his time were activated by Maccabean ideals. To have admitted a positive relationship between the two revolts would have been tantamount to saying that the war against Roman domination was a true expression of Jewish

religious belief. Josephus wished to portray the extremists'
defeat as the judgment of God.

Resistance to Roman rule had grown into a national movement at the start of the revolt, as is indicated by the existence
of several resistance groups, including at least two factions of
Zealots. There were, says Professor K. Schubert, (in *Jewish
Religious Parties and Sects: The Crucible of Christianity*)
'several insurrectionary groups' having in common only the
wish to 'establish by force the absolute Sovereignty of God in
their land against the Romans.'

Deep-rooted national resistance might have smouldered in-
definitely had it not been galvanized by Judas of Galilee.
Josephus records that Judas founded a 'fourth sect' and 'another
system of philosophy', the true name of which, because of its
ancient and honourable past, he is at pains to conceal. These
revolutionaries called themselves *Kanna'im* or Cananaeans, the
'zealous ones', of which the Greek equivalent was the word
Zealotes.

Writing after these Zealots had led his people into what he
considered to have been a suicidal and fatal war of independence, Josephus, like the Romans, calls them bandits and assassins. These *lestai* or criminals, Josephus emphasizes, had nothing
in common with the other three sects he has described—the
Sadducees, Pharisees, and Essenes.

Yet, despite his derogatory words, Josephus supplies information which, when interpreted, provides a very different
picture of these Zealots. Their founder, he admits, was a
'sophist' or a learned Teacher of the Law, a Rabbi. He shows
'that redoubtable doctor', as he calls this leader, to have been a
powerful and significant political figure. He bears grudging and
perhaps unconscious witness to the religious character of the
Zealots' principles, and to the amazing courage with which
they sacrificed themselves for their ideals.

His disparaging epithets were required to disguise from his
Roman leaders that these Zealots were fervent patriots who rose
in revolt, not, as Josephus claims, to commit robbery and
murder, but to fulfil God's commandments. Josephus was not
the only propagandist who sought to absolve his co-religionists

from association with Zealot principles. Writing simultaneously in Rome, the Evangelist Mark concealed the true identity of one of Jesus's intimate band of disciples by calling Simon the 'Cananaean', without explaining as he usually does the meaning of the Aramaic word. Mark also obscured the true character of the two 'thieves' between whom Jesus had been crucified by adopting the denigrating Roman term *lestai* for 'Zealots'.

Mark and Josephus wrote to exonerate their co-religionists from the guilt, in Roman eyes, of having inspired the rebellion. It is a remarkable example of the power of propaganda that, after the destruction of Jerusalem, Judaism retained its status as a *religio licita* or allowed religion, and that twenty years later Luke felt himself free to admit the embarrassing association of his Master with a Zealot disciple, one of the ferocious band of guerilla fighters, a man whose principles had not debarred him from becoming one of Jesus's intimate friends.

Mark's apologetic purpose is less easily discernible than that of Josephus, who succeeded in obscuring the true character of the Zealots for nineteen hundred years. Through our modern knowledge of national resistance movements, we can now see them as uncompromising patriots, the inheritors of a tradition —older than their founder—of resistance to foreign rule as a religious duty. They believed subservience to be disloyalty to God, the absolute sovereign Lord of Israel. For the Zealots, the payment of tribute to a pagan Emperor was a standing insult. It became the burning question, and the test of their loyalty to their principles.

The Galilean Judas, whom Josephus describes as the son of a 'brigand-chieftain' (the term by which he disguises the character of Judas's father, Hezekiah, who had been executed by Herod), appeared first during the disturbances following Herod's death in 4 B.C. As Josephus relates, he

> got together a large number of desperate men at Sephoris in Galilee and there made an assault on the royal palace, and having seized all the arms that were stored there, he armed every single one of his men and made off with all the

22

property that had been seized there. He became an object of terror to all men by plundering those he came across in his desire for great possessions and his ambition for royal rank, a prize that he expected to obtain not through the practice of virtue but through excessive ill-treatment of others.

It may have been about this time that John the Baptist appeared, preaching and baptizing in the wilderness. To place his appearance that early is not inconsistent with Matthew's arrangement of events, and is suggested by the passage which occurs in the Slavonic Manuscripts of Josephus. Why this source of evidence cannot be accepted without corroboration is discussed in Appendix A. According to that source, John's teaching paralleled that of Judas of Galilee, for we read, 'God has sent me to show you the way of the Law, by which ye shall be freed from many tyrants. And no mortal shall rule over you but only the Highest who has sent me.' John stigmatized the conservative sects, the Pharisees and Sadducees, as a 'generation of vipers', a description which suggests that he classed himself as a revolutionary.

Hezekiah and his son Judas each claimed to be, or were recognized as, the Messiah-King, a Jewish concept which had peculiar significance during the period of Roman rule. The meaning of the term became, and has remained, ambiguous and plagued by controversy as later Christian theologians began to interpret the Messianic role of their Jewish founder.

According to the Christian editor of the works of Josephus, H. St J. Thackeray, the first century of our era was marked by the widespread and deep-seated belief, throughout the whole of the East, that a person or persons issuing from Judaea, was destined at that time to rule the world'. And that belief was 'doubtless a main factor in fostering the passionate desire of a large section of the [Jewish] nation for independence, and for promoting the struggle with Rome which ended in catastrophe'. Understandably, the Jews interpreted the oracle to mean a person of their own race, for the Messianic concept was peculiarly Jewish. Two Jewish scholars have written books in an attempt to explain how their first-century ancestors conceived the

Messiah. (J. Klauser, *The Messianic Idea in Israel*, and S. Mowinckel, *He That Cometh*.)

Both authors emphasize that the Messianic concept developed and changed according to historical circumstance. The glorious hope so expressed grew in proportion to the vicissitudes experienced by the Jews. Both scholars discern *two* concepts which, according to Klauser, became merged into one and, in Mowinckel's opinion, never completely fused. The authors agree, however, in asserting that in Roman times the imminence of a Messiah was largely a superstition of the common people, those who suffered most during the occupation and whose visionary hopes were fanned by the popular prophets.

Klauser says:

In the course of the long evolution of the Jewish Messianic idea, two different conceptions were inseparably woven together. These two elements walked arm in arm. The Messiah must be both a *King* and a *Redeemer*. He must overthrow the enemies of Israel, establish the kingdom of Israel, and rebuild the Temple, and at the same time he must reform the world through the Kingdom of God, root out idolatory from the world, proclaim the one and only God to all, put an end to sin, and be wise, pious, and just as no man had been before him or ever would be after him. In short, he is the great political and spiritual hero at one and the same time.

In an earlier book (*Jesus of Nazareth*) Klauser put it thus:

The Jewish Messiah is above all a redeemer of his people from subservience to foreign rulers ... Having been brought up on the popular prophets (unauthorized writings coupled with visionary promises) the popular masses were accustomed to see in every wonder worker and preacher, a prospective saviour and ruler, a King and a Messiah, a supernatural political saviour and a spiritual saviour filled with the divine spirit.

Klauser remarks that Josephus attests the political significance of the Messiah, and it is not inopportune to recall here that the disciples chose the moment of Jesus's apparent reappearance from the dead to inquire whether it was his intention 'at this time' to 'restore the kingdom of Israel'.

Mowinckel considers that the 'transcendental' otherworldly Messiah was not of Jewish origin, and that, in the first century, amongst the Jewish masses the 'this-worldly' national future hope concept prevailed:

It appealed directly to popular sentiment and aspirations, particularly in evil times, when feelings ran high, because of the pressure of alien rule, social and economic difficulties, and the reaction against the breach of ancient custom by the 'Hellenists' and foreigners, and their outrage of religious feeling. It was also amongst the masses of the people that this older, this worldly conception of the Messiah lived on.

Mowinckel says that 'the Messiah would be primarily a royal deliverer, the enemy of Rome—a Zealot'.

Judas of Galilee and Jesus both preached the absolute sovereignty of God, and forbade the payment of tribute to a pagan Emperor, at the time when the Jewish masses fervently believed that 'the time is at hand', and the Kingdom of God imminent. At the moment of crisis the Messiah would appear at the head of legions of angels. Those who had given their lives to establish the Kingdom of Heaven would rise from the dead to share in its benefits.

If, as some scholars think (C. Roth, *The Historical Background of the Dead Sea Scrolls*, and C. R. Driver, *The Judaean Scrolls*), it was the Zealots, rather than the Essenes, who reoccupied the monastery at Qumran in A.D. 6, following its abandonment in 31 B.C. as the result of a disastrous earthquake, the Dead Sea Scrolls may represent Zealot beliefs. The concurrence of the founding of Zealotism, and its immediate disappearance 'underground' circa A.D. 6, with the re-occupation of the lonely site disclosed by archaeology is remarkable. The monastery was later destroyed by the Romans in A.D. 68–70, when the Scrolls were concealed in caves in the cliffs above; it was re-occupied by resistance fighters, who may have been Zealots, in A.D. 132. The theory that the Scrolls belonged to the Zealots has received considerable support from the discovery of fragments of similar Scrolls at Masada, the Zealot stronghold farther down the Dead Sea. The Roman historian Pliny the Elder, who campaigned with General Titus, wrote in A.D. 77 (*Historia Naturalia* V. XVIII, 73) that the Essenes lived near the west coast of the Dead Sea, but far enough away to avoid its noxious exhalations—'above En-gedi', [Engaddi] a spot between Qumran and Masada. They were living there unmolested, then, after Jerusalem and Masada had fallen, in the defence of which the fierce Zealots had died. If the Essenes had believed in the message of the war-like Scrolls, presumably they would have died with them. The monastery at Qumran, as I saw during my visit to the Holy Land before writing this, stands on a ledge within a few hundred yards of the sea of 'dangerous exhalations'. With a handy escape route up the cleft to the hills above, it would have made an excellent hideout for guerilla fighters.

But the identification of the Zealots with Qumran, and with the Scrolls, is too controversial, because of the ambiguous nature of the texts, to prove Scroll ownership decisively. One of the Scrolls, *The War of the Sons of Light Against the Sons of Darkness*, describes the final war of Armaggedon against the Romans, and envisages its outcome as pre-ordained by God. Another, *The Manual of Discipline*, appears to reflect the Zealot code as it was defined by Judas of Galilee. He escaped the fate of the two thousand rebels crucified by Varus, the Roman Legate of Syria, who brought three legions to suppress the insurrections occasioned by the death of Herod in 4 B.C. Ten years later Judas reappeared and, as Josephus describes in *Concerning the Jewish War*, 'incited his countrymen to revolt, upbraiding them as cowards for consenting to pay tribute to the Romans and tolerating mortal masters, after having God for their Lord'.

Writing in later life when he may have felt that the Romans had forgotten the dangerous implications of Zealotism, Josephus supplies a longer account in his *Antiquities*. The Jews, although shocked to hear of the registration of property, gradually yielded to the arguments of the High Priest Jozar:

But a certain Judas, a Gaulanite from a city named Gamala, who had enlisted the aid of Zaddock, a Pharisee, threw himself into the cause of rebellion. They said that the assessment carried with it a status amounting to downright slavery no less, and appealed to the nation to make a bid for independence. They urged that in case of success the Jews would have laid the foundation of prosperity, while if they failed to obtain any such boon, they would win honour and renown for their lofty aim; and that Heaven would be their zealous helper to no lesser end than the furthering of their enterprises until it succeeded—all the more if with high devotion in their hearts they stood firm and did not shrink from the bloodshed that might be necessary. Since the populace, when they heard their appeals, responded gladly, the plot to strike boldly made serious progress.

These Zealots, states Josephus, sowed the seeds of strife between the Jewish factions, and the slaughter of their fellow citizens.

Judas and Zaddok started among us an intrusive fourth school of philosophy; and when they had won an abundance of devotees, they filled the body politic immediately with tumult, also planting the seeds of those troubles which subsequently overtook it, all because of the novelty of this hitherto unknown philosophy that I shall now describe. My reason for giving this brief account of it is chiefly that the zeal which Judas and Zaddok inspired in the younger element meant the ruin of our cause.

Having described the three other religious sects, Josephus continues:

As for the fourth of the philosophies, Judas the Galilean set himself up as leader of it. This school agrees in all other respects with the opinions of the Pharisees, except that they have a passion for liberty that is almost unconquerable, since they are convinced that God alone is their leader and master. They think little of submitting to death in unusual

27

forms and permitting vengeance to fall on kinsmen and friends if only they may avoid calling any man master. Inasmuch as most people have seen the steadfastness of their resolution amid such circumstances, I may forego any further account. For I have no fear that anything reported of them will be considered incredible. The danger is, rather, that report may minimize the indifference with which they accept the grinding misery of pain.

In these passages Josephus identifies the Zealots as the fomenters of rebellion, bears witness to their ideals and courage, associates Judas with a Pharisee named Zaddok, and states that the profession of Zealotism was not incompatible with Pharisaic principles, which to Josephus were the highest attainable. His unguarded statements indicate that these sectarians were not self-seeking brigands and murderers, as Josephus probably hoped the Romans would believe.

The Jews, says Josephus, responded gladly to Judas's appeal, and his plot to strike boldly made serious progress. But Josephus fails to remark the fate of Judas, a strange omission which is remedied by the statement of the Rabbi Gamaliel, recorded in *Acts* (5:37) in reference to the careers of various Messiahs: '[there] rose up Judas of Galilee in the days of the enrolment, and drew away some of the people after him; he also perished and all, as many as obeyed him, were scattered abroad'.

Zealotism did not die with its founder. Judas's followers continued their subversive activities, applying to would-be Messiahs the test, the crucial question, as to whether or not it was lawful to pay tribute to Caesar.

Three

The
Roman Procurators

Prophet, priest, sandalmaker, waterseller, street-sweeper, carpenter, well-digger, husbandman, day labourer, merchant, scrivener, rich man, poor man—every Jew had become the subject of a race of unsentimental, harsh realists who, if they so willed, could reduce him to abject poverty, exterminate him or drive him from his Holy Land. The Jews at the beginning of the first century had no knowledge that, within 135 years, after two bloody rebellions, the wretched survivors of their nation would be driven forth to wander the face of the earth for eighteen centuries. Nor could they know that, soon after A.D. 70, a learned Rabbi, wandering disconsolately over the ruins of the Temple, would spot a fox creeping from the debris of what had once been the Holy of Holies, the abode of God Himself.

Intransigent, uncompromising, obstinate, driven by the unconquerable will of the human spirit, the Jews preferred to die rather than acknowledge a mortal master. God, they fervently believed, would deliver them. As the hardships of alien rule became harsher, more and more people deserted the pacific philosophy of the Pharisees, who were content to await the fulfillment of God's purpose, and joined the bellicose insurgents.

The Roman yoke ground hardest upon the common people who bore the burden of taxation. Their taxes, added to their temple dues and the extortions of the Procurators as well as of their own priestly aristocracy, kept them in dire poverty. Then, as now, Palestine was a harsh land from which to gain a living. It supported in the first century no greater number of people, probably, than in 1926, when the population numbered 500,000. Of these, about 50,000 lived in Jerusalem. Its population was swollen thrice annually by the influx of pilgrims, who at the Passover may have numbered 125,000.

THE MACCABEAN RULERS OF PALESTINE

165 – 37 B.C.

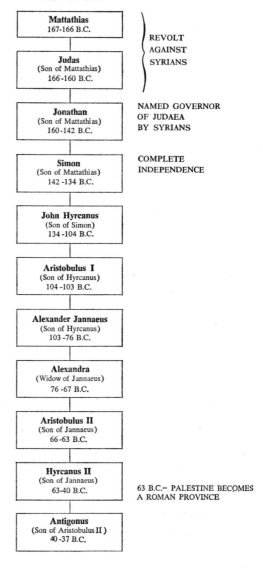

Mattathias
167-166 B.C.

Judas
(Son of Mattathias)
166-160 B.C.

REVOLT
AGAINST
SYRIANS

Jonathan
(Son of Mattathias)
160-142 B.C.

NAMED GOVERNOR
OF JUDAEA
BY SYRIANS

Simon
(Son of Mattathias)
142 -134 B.C.

COMPLETE
INDEPENDENCE

John Hyrcanus
(Son of Simon)
134 -104 B.C.

Aristobulus I
(Son of Hyrcanus)
104 -103 B.C.

Alexander Jannaeus
(Son of Hyrcanus)
103 -76 B.C.

Alexandra
(Widow of Jannaeus)
76 -67 B.C.

Aristobulus II
(Son of Jannaeus)
66 -63 B.C.

Hyrcanus II
(Son of Jannaeus)
63-40 B.C.

63 B.C.– PALESTINE BECOMES
A ROMAN PROVINCE

Antigonus
(Son of Aristobulus II)
40 -37 B.C.

GOVERNMENT OF PALESTINE

55 B.C. - 70 A.D.

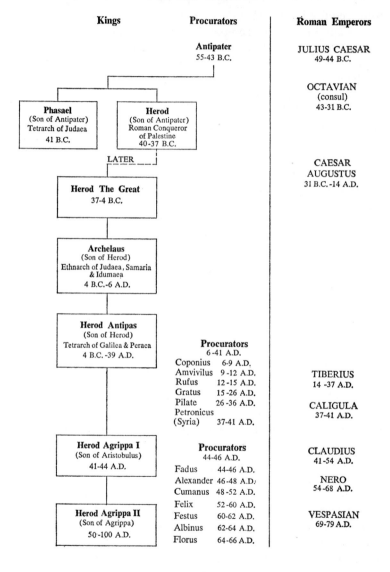

Kings	Procurators	Roman Emperors
	Antipater 55-43 B.C.	JULIUS CAESAR 49-44 B.C.
		OCTAVIAN (consul) 43-31 B.C.
Phasael (Son of Antipater) Tetrarch of Judaea 41 B.C.	**Herod** (Son of Antipater) Roman Conqueror of Palestine 40-37 B.C.	
LATER		CAESAR AUGUSTUS 31 B.C.-14 A.D.
Herod The Great 37-4 B.C.		
Archelaus (Son of Herod) Ethnarch of Judaea, Samaria & Idumaea 4 B.C.-6 A.D.		
Herod Antipas (Son of Herod) Tetrarch of Galilea & Peraea 4 B.C. -39 A.D.	**Procurators** 6-41 A.D. Coponius 6-9 A.D. Amvivilus 9 -12 A.D. Rufus 12 -15 A.D. Gratus 15 -26 A.D. Pilate 26 -36 A.D. Petronicus (Syria) 37-41 A.D.	TIBERIUS 14 -37 A.D. CALIGULA 37-41 A.D.
Herod Agrippa I (Son of Aristobulus) 41-44 A.D.	**Procurators** 44-46 A.D. Fadus 44-46 A.D. Alexander 46-48 A.D. Cumanus 48 -52 A.D.	CLAUDIUS 41-54 A.D. NERO 54-68 A.D.
Herod Agrippa II (Son of Agrippa) 50-100 A.D.	Felix 52 -60 A.D. Festus 60-62 A.D. Albinus 62-64 A.D. Florus 64-66 A.D.	VESPASIAN 69-79 A.D.

The performance of religious rites and the maintenance of the Temple required the services of about 7,200 priests and 9,600 Levites or priestly servants. One hundred doorkeepers were required each night to close the massive Temple doors. The Captain of the Temple Police, the *Sagan*, was next in rank to the single High Priest, to whom he was always closely related.

The priests and Levites were divided into 'courses'. When not on duty, they pursued ordinary occupations throughout the country, as did the Scribes and Rabbis—the interpreters of the Law or 'theologians' as we may describe them. The Rabbis, many of whom were very poor, were held in high esteem. Only craftsmen at their work were exempted from the rule that all must rise to their feet as these learned men passed by.

The priests conducted the Temple rites according to Pharasaic interpretation of the Law, frequently to the irritation of the Sadducean high-priestly caste, made up of families who had held that office by hereditary right until the Roman occupation. The appointment of High Priests became a bone of contention, sometimes under the control of the Jews and sometimes made at the whim of a particular Roman Procurator. Several of the latter took the precaution, to prevent unauthorized election, of withholding the priestly vestments, lacking which the High Priest could not enter the Holy of Holies on the Day of Atonement. Roman choice of their representative with God, and Roman custody of his ceremonial robe, exemplified to the Jews their degrading dependence on alien masters. But up to the Siege of Jerusalem the Romans never deprived the Jews of control of their own civil and religious law courts, at the apex of which stood the Sanhedrin. This, the 'council of Seventy', included the Sadducees and learned Pharisees, and was controlled by the leading lay families and the High Priests—a term denoting both current and past holders of that office.

Carefully chosen from the close-knit families who claimed the hereditary right of appointment, the High Priests, though unpaid, reaped a rich reward. They controlled the Temple Treasury, which served as a National Bank, and the markets within the Temple walls where the sacrificial beasts had to be bought, and where foreign currency was exchanged for Jewish shekels. Foreign and Roman coins were brought there both by native pilgrims and by those who had travelled from the widespread Diaspora—the colonies of Jews who lived throughout the Roman and Parthian Empires.

The Jews in 'Babylonia', as Mesopotamia was still called, comprised the descendants of the Israelites exiled at various times—in 722 B.C., between 597 and 586 B.C., and in 346 B.C. Many Jews also lived in Syria and in the cities of Asia Minor. Those who congregated in Rome and Alexandria, the chief centres of the Dispersion, were descendants of freed slaves or of Jews who had emigrated for commercial purposes. Josephus estimated that at the death of Herod 8,000 Jews lived in Rome. Many more dwelt in Alexandria, whose Jewish population early in the first century has been estimated at 200,000. In both cities the Jews had formed close-knit communities accorded extraordinary privileges by the Romans, which they enjoyed despite the popular antagonism caused by Jewish exclusiveness. Of all peoples subject to the Romans, only the Jews were permitted to opt out of the State Cult. They were also exempted from military service because of their strict dietary laws and absolute refusal to work on the Sabbath. They were also freed from attending courts of law on that day. And they were allowed to transfer annually to Jerusalem large sums in gold with which to pay their Temple dues, even when such transfers jeopardized the Roman 'balance of payments'.

For reasons difficult to understand, the Romans pampered Jews who preferred to live outside Palestine. This amicable relationship was traditional, dating in Alexandria back to the privileges conferred by Alexander the Great. In Rome the cordial friendship began when the Jews supported Julius Caesar in his bid for power and mourned his death, as Suetonius describes. Throughout the Empire, and especially in Rome and Alexandria, the Jews appeared to have gained by that intransigence which in Palestine eventually cost them their Promised Land. They refused to be assimilated, and the practical Romans, it seems, found it wiser to humour them than risk disorders which, in their widespread dispersion, might cause trouble throughout the Empire. Roman policy on the Jewish problem remained reasonably constant and proved useful in A.D. 66, when on the outbreak of revolt in Palestine the Diaspora remained quiet. The threat to the national religion, and expectation of divine aid, failed to rouse those Jews whose life abroad had taught them a certain independence.

Roman rule in Judaea began in earnest in A.D. 6 with the arrival of the first Procurator, Coponius, when his superior, Quirinius, took the strange step of deposing the High Priest Jozar, who had, according to Josephus, urged submission to the hated Census. As is so often his way, Josephus is irritatingly vague about the reason for Jozar's dismissal. He says only that 'since the high-priest Jozar had now been overpowered by a popular faction, Quirinius stripped him of the dignity of his office, and installed Ananus, the son of Seth, as high-priest'. Perhaps Jozar had served his purpose—and his consequent unpopularity had certainly jeopardized his usefulness.

Between A.D. 9, the year of Coponius's recall, and A.D. 26, Roman rule was served by three further Procurators, the last of whom, Valerius Gratus, appointed during his eleven-year term of office no less than four High Priests, culminating with Caiaphas, who was retained by Pontius Pilate throughout his own procuratorship. Procurators were minor Roman officials, drawn from the middle class. Though usually no more than a kind of financial officer, the Procurator, or governor, of a minor province received the rank of *Praefectus*. He controlled a force of auxiliary troops, which in Palestine numbered about three thousand, mainly of Syrian origin. Caesarea on the coast became the official Roman capital, and the Procurators avoided Jerusalem, going there only at times of trouble. A cohort commanded by a Tribune occupied the Antonia fortress which overlooked the Temple. Galilee remained until A.D. 39 under the direct rule of Herod's son Antipas, who, like the Procurator of Judaea, was responsible to the Legate of Syria and to the Emperor of Rome for the tranquillity of his kingdom. Both Tetrarch and Procurator became the servants of a new Emperor when, in A.D. 14, Augustus was succeeded by Tiberius. Five years later the new Emperor banished the Jews temporarily from Rome, an incident reported by Josephus in his *Antiquities*.

The story of the Roman scandals which led to the expulsion of the Jewish community would, in the ordinary way, have no bearing on the theme of this book; it takes on importance because of the order in which Josephus narrates his *Antiquities*. He places his stories of the matrons Paulina and Fulvia, whose misfortunes occurred in A.D. 19, after he has already made some mention of the would-be Messiah Jesus, whose brief appearance probably took place some time after A.D. 26, the year of Pilate's arrival in Judaea—a confusion which has not escaped notice.

The expulsion of the Jews and other foreigners from Rome, it appears, did not affect their status within the Empire. It was ordered as a disciplinary action intended to curb the over-eagerness in conversion, and to keep down the growing concentration in Rome of a number of Oriental cults. These were becoming too popular, particularly among women, to the detriment of the national religion: the worship of the divine Emperor by which the Romans bound together their scattered Empire. The imperial wrath fell also upon the devotees of the cult of Isis, and upon the foreign astrologers and magicians from whom the aristocracy sought signs and revelations, particularly those that pointed to the early demise of the unpopular Tiberius.

Josephus's first story relates to the noble and wealthy lady Paulina, whom he describes as having 'a comely appearance, and was at an age at which women are most exuberant'. Nonetheless, she was highly virtuous, devoting her life to good conduct. The lively manner in which Josephus tells the story indicates his enjoyment of the gossip which had survived until A.D. 64, when he visited Rome.

> She was married to Saturnius, who was fully a match for her in reputation. Decius Mundus, who ranked high among the knights of his day, was in love with her. When he saw that her character was too strong to succumb to gifts, since, even when he sent them abundantly, she scorned them, his passion was inflamed all the more, so that he actually promised to give her 200,000 Attic drachmas if he could share her bed a single time. When even this failed to shake her

resolution, he, finding it intolerable not to win his suit, thought that it would be fitting to condemn himself to death by starvation and thus to put an end to the suffering that had overtaken him. And so he decided upon such a death and was actually proceeding to carry out his resolve. Mundus, however, had a freed-woman named Ida, expert in every kind of mischief, whom his father had emancipated. She had no patience with the young man's resolve to die, for it was obvious what he intended. She went to him, used argument to rouse him, and by plausibly undertaking to find a way, held out hope that he might succeed in enjoying intimate relations with Paulina. When he joyfully listened to her importunity, she informed him that she would require no more than 50,000 drachmas to secure the woman. These proposals encouraged the youth, and she received the sum for which she had asked. She did not, however, proceed by the same course as had previous agents, since she perceived that this woman would never succumb to bribes. But knowing that the lady was very much given to the worship of Isis, Ida devised the following stratagem. She had an interview with some of the priests and promised them every assurance, above all, a sum of money amounting to 25,000 drachmas payable at once and as much more after the success of the plot. She then explained the young man's passionate desire for the woman and urged them to bend every effort to secure her for him. The impact of the money was enough to sway them, and they agreed. The eldest of them hastened to Paulina's house and, on being admitted, requested a private talk with her. This being accorded, he said that he had been sent to her by the god Anubis; the god had fallen in love with her and bade her come to him. The message was what she would most have wished. Not only did she pride herself among her lady friends on receiving such an invitation from Anubis, but she told her husband of her summons to dine with and share the bed of Anubis. Her husband concurred, since he had no doubt of his wife's chastity. Go then she did to the temple. After supper, when it came time to sleep, the doors within the shrine were shut by the priest and the lamps were cleared away. Mundus, for he had been concealed there beforehand, was not rebuffed when he sought intercourse with her. Indeed it was a nightlong service that she performed for him, assuming that he was the god. He departed before the priests, who had been informed of the scheme, had begun to stir. Paulina went early in the morning to her husband and described in detail the divine manifestations of Anubis, and before the ladies, her friends, she put on great airs in talking about him. Those who heard, having regard to the substance of the matter, were incredulous; and yet, on the other hand, finding it impossible not to believe her when they took into consideration her chastity and position in society, they were reduced to marvelling. Two days after the incident, Mundus put himself in her way and said: 'Well, Paulina, you have saved me 200,000 drachmas which you could have added to your estate, yet you have rendered to perfection the service I urged you to perform. As for your attempt to flout Mundus, I did not concern myself about names, though I did about the pleasure to be derived from the act, so I adopted the name of Anubis as my own.' With these words he departed. Then she, being now aware for the first time of his dastardly deed, rent her garment; and when she had disclosed to her husband the enormity of the scheme, she begged him not to neglect to obtain redress. He in turn brought the matter to the notice of the emperor. When Tiberius had fully informed himself by examining the priests, he crucified both them and Ida, for the hellish thing was her doing and it was she who had contrived the whole plot against the lady's honour. Moreover, he razed the temple and ordered the statue of Isis to be cast into the Tiber River. Mundus' sentence was exile, since Tiberius regarded the fact that his crime had been committed under the influence of passion as a bar to a more severe penalty. Such were the insolent acts of the priests in the temple of Isis.

Josephus's second story directly concerns a Jew, a 'complete scoundrel who had fled his own country because he was accused of transgressing certain laws and feared punishment on that account'. Enlisting three confederates, no better in character than himself, this man urged Fulvia, a woman of high rank who had become a convert to Judaism, to send purple and gold to the Temple at Jerusalem, gifts which the conspirators appropriated. Fulvia's husband, a friend of the Emperor's, reported to Tiberius how his wife had been defrauded, whereupon he ordered the Jews to leave Rome. Dio Cassius, the Roman historian, says that Jewish proselytes were included in the punishment unless they recanted, a statement which suggests the true cause of banishment.

Four thousand Jews of Rome were then drafted for military service and sent to suppress brigandage in Sardinia; the conscripts steadfastly refused to defile themselves by eating army food and declined to work on the Sabbath. Many failed to survive the rigours of the island's unhealthy climate, a circumstance that brought from the historian Tacitus the callous remark 'Who cared?' The remainder were eventually allowed to return to Rome, where we shall hear of them again.

Tiberius reigned from A.D. 14 to A.D. 37, a period when, according to Tacitus, 'all was quiet' in Palestine. Josephus, on the other hand, refers to three incidents during Pilate's governorship which suggest that Jewish resistance to foreign rule was growing.

Four

Emperor Tiberius
and Pilate

By his statement in the *Antiquities* that Pilate was recalled to
Rome in A.D. 36, after ten years as Procurator of Judaea, Josephus implies that he began his term of office in A.D. 26. The
latter date, however, conflicts with the order of other events
recorded in that book. Some scholars maintain that Pilate may
have reached Judaea as early as A.D. 18. The considerable
length of Pilate's governorship, whatever it may have been,
illustrates the Emperor Tiberius's 'dilatory character', as Josephus calls it, and provides insight into Roman methods of
provincial administration.

Tiberius was never in a hurry, explains the historian, to re-
place Procurators unless they died at their posts, and when he
was asked why he was so slow in such matters, Tiberius replied
that he allowed these officials to remain in office out of consideration for the feelings of the subject people. He explained
that 'it was a law of nature that governors are prone to engage
in extortion'. When appointments were short, the spur to
peculation was even greater. If, on the contrary, they kept their
posts longer, he said, they would become glutted with their
spoils and grow sluggish in pursuing new ones. To illustrate his
point, Tiberius told a fable, according to Josephus:

Once a man lay wounded, and a swarm of flies hovered
about his wounds. A passer-by took pity on his evil plight,
and, in the belief that he did not raise a hand because he
could not, was about to step up and shoo them off. The
wounded man, however, begged him to think no more of
doing anything about it. At this the man spoke up and
asked him why he was not interested in escaping from his
wretched condition. 'Why,' said he, 'you would put me in

a worse position if you drove them off. For since these flies have already had their fill of blood, they no longer feel such a pressing need to annoy me but are in some measure slack. But if others were to come with a fresh appetite, they would take over my now weakened body and that would indeed be the death of me.'

Josephus points to the record of Tiberius's acts to bear out his account of the Emperor's humour about such matters:

For during the twenty-two years that he was emperor he sent altogether two men, Gratus and Pilate, his successor, to govern the Jewish nation. Nor did he behave so only when he dealt with the Jews; he was no different with his other subjects. Moreover, as for his procrastination in hearing the cases of prisoners, he explained that this was because an immediate hearing would alleviate the present miseries of those condemned to death, whereas they did not deserve to meet with such luck. When, however, they were kept waiting, the weight of their misfortune was rendered more severe by the vexation which was laid upon them.

Whatever the extent of his extortions, Pontius Pilate exasperated his subjects by his tactless acts as well. He inflamed further their desire for independence, which the conciliatory policy of his predecessors, who had avoided flouting Jewish religious susceptibilities, may have kept in abeyance.

Pilate's disregard for Jewish feelings was evident when he brought into Jerusalem imperial standards showing the Emperor's face, thus violating the Jewish aversion for images. (Until then the Roman soldiers had left them behind when they entered the Holy City.) Josephus fails to explain whether Pilate acted on orders from Rome, or on his own initiative. Attractive as the latter explanation may seem, it is unlikely that he would have reversed established practice unless he simply enjoyed antagonizing the Jews. He was 'unwilling to do anything acceptable' in their regard, according to the contemporary Jewish philosopher Philo, who describes Pilate as a man of inflexible disposition, merciless and obstinate, and of ferocious passions. Josephus, too, depicts Pilate as cruel and contemptuous of the Jews. (This combined testimony is completely at variance with the weak, vacillating character depicted in the Gospels.)

It is much more probable, however, that Tiberius, goaded by his adviser Sejanus, who was noted for his anti-Jewish sentiments, decided the change of policy: the Jews were to be brought into line with other subject peoples, by being forced to accept the offensive imperial insignia. It was an unwise move and one which played into the hands of the extremists.

Although his account of the Roman Standards incident in the *Antiquities* is the longer, Josephus gave its pith in the *Jewish War*:

Pilate, being sent by Tiberius as procurator to Judaea, introduced into Jerusalem by night and under cover the effigies of Caesar which are called standards. This proceeding, when day broke, aroused immense excitement among the Jews; those on the spot were in consternation, considering their laws to have been trampled under foot, as those laws permit no image to be erected in the city; while the indignation of the townspeople stirred the country-folks, who flocked together in crowds. Hastening after Pilate to Caesarea, the Jews implored him to remove the standards from Jerusalem and to uphold the laws of their ancestors. When Pilate refused, they fell prostrate around his house and for five whole days and nights remained motionless in that position.

On the ensuing day Pilate took his seat on his tribunal in the great stadium and summoning the multitude, with the apparent intention of answering them, gave the arranged signal to his armed soldiers to surround the Jews. Finding themselves in a ring of troops, three deep, the Jews were struck dumb at this unexpected sight. Pilate, after threatening to cut them down, if they refused to admit Caesar's image, signalled to the soldiers to draw their swords. Thereupon the Jews, as by concerted action, flung themselves in a body on the ground, extended their necks, and exclaimed that they were ready rather to die than to transgress the law. Overcome with astonishment at such intense religious zeal, Pilate gave orders for the immediate removal of the standards from Jerusalem.

The *Antiquities* version has it that at first Pilate refused to yield 'since to do so would be an outrage to the Emperor', a remark which suggests that the governor had complied with an official order and later reversed it on his own judgment. Josephus is at pains to emphasize that the Jews reacted to the threat to their religion in an orderly and peaceful manner, in contrast, perhaps, to the more violent reaction of the Zealots, which Josephus neglects to mention.

Philo relates a similar challenge to Jewish beliefs in Pilate's introduction of gilded shields into Jerusalem's royal palace. (These shields bore inscriptions, not images.) Once again the Jews objected, travelled the sixty miles to Caesarea, and, led by four Herodian princes, challenged Pilate to produce his authority. They also threatened to write to Tiberius. Fearing that his maladministration would come to light, says Philo, Pilate climbed down.

Pilate's actions did not result, as far as we know, in censure, which suggests that his reversal of orders was accepted by Tiberius. Nonetheless, states Philo, the Emperor was furiously angry. Bewildered as they may have been by the depth of Jewish intransigence, the Romans had been forced to yield. Their success encouraged and strengthened the Jews, for when, in A.D. 37, Vitelius, the Legate of Syria, went to make war on Aretas, the Arabian king, he was persuaded to march his legions outside Judaea to avoid wounding Jewish susceptibilities by the display of the offending regimental symbols.

Vitelius's mission was to punish Aretas for defeating Antipas, the Tetrarch of Galilee. He had incurred Aretas's wrath by divorcing his daughter. Antipas had also incurred the wrath of the Jews by marrying in her stead Herodias, his deceased brother Philip's wife, in defiance of Jewish Law. John the Baptist publicly rebuked Antipas, and was executed at the instigation of Herodias. Josephus's interpretation of the Baptist's death differs from that of the Bible in attributing the execution to John's preaching, which the Tetrarch feared might lead to sedition and cause an uprising. This suggests that John's message was political rather than religious. Jesus, we recall, is reputed to have declared that the Baptist was the first to attempt to bring about the realization of the Kingdom of Heaven: 'From the days of the Baptist, the Kingdom of Heaven suffered violence, and the men of violence take it by force.' The term 'Kingdom of Heaven' implied a state of freedom from alien rule.

Pilate again exasperated the Jews, provoking a fresh uproar, as Josephus records, by expending Temple funds to construct an aqueduct. This was the sort of programme by which avaricious governors feathered their nests.

> Indignant at this proceeding, the populace formed a ring round the tribunal of Pilate, then on a visit to Jerusalem, and besieged him with angry clamour. He, foreseeing the tumult, had interspersed among the crowd a troop of his soldiers, armed but disguised in civilian dress, with orders not to use their swords, but to beat any rioters with cudgels. He now from the tribunal gave the agreed signal. Large numbers of the Jews perished, some from the blows which they received, others trodden to death by their companions in the ensuing flight. Cowed by the fate of the victims, the multitude was reduced to silence.

Though Pilate's attempt to bring water into Jerusalem, inadequately served by a single spring, at the Pool of Siloam which lay within the city walls, may seem laudable, the method Pilate employed to finance the enterprise—seizing the sacred treasure, the 'gifts given to God'—infuriated the Jews. Josephus states, in *Antiquities*, 'this ended the uprising'. The work on the aqueduct appears to have been carried out, for archaeological excavation has disclosed, on the west of the city, two ancient conduits, the lower of which conforms to an aqueduct of the Roman period.

Pilate's career in Judaea was brought to a sudden end in the year A.D. 36–37. He found himself faced by an armed crowd of Samaritans, persuaded by a minor prophet that he could show them the sacred vessels hidden by Moses on Mount Gerizim. Pilate dispersed them with great slaughter. Samaritan protests to the Legate of Syria led to Pilate's recall to Rome.

The other disturbance which occurred during Pilate's governorship requires a separate chapter.

Five

The
Messiah Jesus

On the outbreak of revolt in A.D. 66, Jesus's onetime disciples, or their associates the 'Fathers of the Jerusalem Church', joined their co-religionists in the struggle for national independence and perished with them. This claim, to be discussed in due course, requires a reassessment of the role of Jesus, who was executed by Pilate as the 'King of the Jews', about the year A.D. 30, the exact date being impossible to determine. Jesus, it seems, was at least sympathetic to Zealotism. (Later Christian apologetic, expressly designed to detach him from his national *milieu* and to dissociate him from the Jewish nationalistic cause in order to allay Roman antagonism to the new religion, denied this.) In Jerusalem he became involved in an insurrection which his triumphal entry may have provoked.

Jesus has been described as an 'inexhaustible subject enthusiastically pursued'. To understand his career, we need to reject the emotional appeal of the Gospel story and to clear up misunderstanding about the role of the Messiah.

As the scholars Klauser and Mowinckel have shown (Chapter II) there were two divergent concepts of the Messiah, that of the political saviour and that of the tragic visionary. Christian theology confuses the two concepts, since the authors of the Gospels wished to disguise the unpalatable fact that the founder of their religion had been put to death by the Romans for political sedition. These authors were also ignorant of, or wilfully misrepresented, contemporary Jewish Messianic and nationalistic hopes.

In their anxiety to show that Jesus was blameless of the charge of treason, the Evangelists falsely represented the contemporary scene, so necessary for a true understanding of him. Nothing in his recorded sayings shows him to have been other than an orthodox Jew; indeed he said that he came not to destroy the Law but to fulfil it. He differed from the strict Pharisees only in the *interpretation* of Jewish Law. He accepted the fervent apocalyptic hopes of the mass of the people.

The contradiction between the contemporary Jewish and the later Christian conception of the Messiah arises from the Christian determination to misinterpret the term. Christians cannot accept, as did the Jews, that 'Messiah' meant an early champion —a human being. The attribution of divinity to a Messiah would have been repugnant to orthodox Jews. They envisaged him, rather, though filled with the divine spirit, leading them to victory in an earthly war to purge their Holy Land of pagan foreigners. In that war the Hosts of Heaven and the human armies would march shoulder to shoulder; the heroes who died would, at final victory, rise from the dead in spirit and in body —the belief that explains the Jews' amazing heroism and willingness to suffer and die for their holy cause.

By his many signs, his 'acts of salvation', Jesus excited Messianic hopes, and his Messianic entry into Jerusalem satisfied those hopes; he probably really expected that God would send His heavenly hosts, that the war would be won without earthly strife. 'Thinkest thou that I cannot now pray to my Father, and he shall presently give me more than twelve legions of angels?' he asked his disciples at the moment of crisis. Final disillusionment came on the Cross, with his last despairing cry: 'My God, my God, why hast thou forsaken me?'

Therein lay the tragedy of Jesus and his people. The exalted hopes of the Jews were vain. They had pinned their faith on God's aid. Their zeal was not enough, for their faith had no foundation.

The inaccuracy of the Christian calendar, not devised until the sixth century, makes the date of Jesus's birth uncertain, but he, was probably born before the death of King Herod in 4 B.C. Jesus grew up in Galilee, the breeding ground of Zealotism, of which he could not have been unaware. He lived in a period of tension and violence, and of fervent apocalyptic hope—the context of the contemporary scene about which the authors of the Gospels are suspiciously silent. Their Jesus seems completely oblivious to the aspirations of his people and unconcerned with their violent reaction to Roman rule. Yet the Gospel writers, telling their story outside Palestine after a lapse of forty years and more, retain hints, derived from Palestinian tradition too strong to be ignored, of disorders and of insurrection in Jerusalem at the time of Jesus's triumphal entry. In unequivocal terms, Jesus proclaimed himself the Messiah-King, the long awaited Saviour who would free his people from foreign rule and establish the Kingdom of Heaven. Jesus could not have been unaware that his role would be literally interpreted by the masses who lived in fervent expectation of this very eventuality.

Jesus's message paralleled that announced by Judas of Galilee, who had preached the absolute sovereignty of God and forbidden the payment of tribute to foreigners. With even greater urgency Jesus taught that 'the time is fulfilled, and the Kingdom of Heaven is at hand'. Its establishment required the overthrow of Roman rule. He condemned the payment of tribute, stating his views in terms which were not at all ambiguous, though the authors of the Gospels would have us believe them so. His famous answer to the question (the basic test of loyalty to the Zealot cause) as to whether or not it was lawful to pay tribute to Caesar, was emphatically stated in terms which to his interrogators were abundantly clear. Jesus did not evade the issue; he told his questioners to 'render unto God' the things that were His—the produce of the Holy Land—and to Caesar the things that were his—the Roman coins that bore his image. In the Gospels Jesus's apparently prudent answer is clearly slanted to imply (to the Romans) that he avoided involvement in a dangerous political issue and, in fact, attested his loyalty to Rome. Yet, the same Gospels admit that one of the accusations which Jesus did not deny at his trial, was that he had 'forbidden' the payment of tribute, a clear act of sedition.

Several other Gospel admissions indicate that Jesus became deeply involved in the nationalistic aspirations of his people, and that he was exclusively Jewish in his outlook. His saying, 'Give not that which is holy to dogs, neither cast your pearls before swine' ('dogs' and 'swine' were scornful Jewish terms for Gentiles), must have been hard words for the Evangelists to

47

stomach, especially as Jesus had ordered his disciples to 'go not into any way of the Gentiles'.

Early in his career, Jesus seems to have been unsure of his role, or unwilling to accept it. Nothing he is recorded as saying in Galilee was sufficiently antagonistic to have brought on him the alleged hatred of the Jewish leaders, shown plotting to destroy him, or to have alarmed the Romans. It is evident that, after initial success, his mission ended in failure, for the excited crowds, which on one occasion 'wanted to take him by force and make him king', melted away, and even some of his disciples drew back, forcing him to ask the Twelve, 'Will you also go away?' 'Think not that I came to cast peace on earth; I came not to cast peace but a sword,' Jesus announced. Provocative words may have been those most acceptable to the masses, who saw in every preacher a potential Messiah, and to his disciples, one of whom was a Zealot.

Mark, as we have seen, calls the disciple Simon the 'Cananaean' (Aramaic for Zealot) without explaining the term. Luke recognizes Simon's identity. Simon (not to be confused with Simon Peter) may not have been the only nationalist among Jesus's intimate band; others may have been Zealot sympathizers, as some of their nicknames suggest. The brothers James and John are called *Boanerges*, which Mark explains to mean 'Sons of Thunder'. But it might imply 'sons of tumult or riot', an interpretation supported by their desire to destroy a village of unco-operative Samaritans. Jesus's chief lieutenant, Simon Peter, is called *Barjonah*. This may identify him as the 'son of Jonah' or, equally well, as one of the *Barjonim*—those who stood outside the law—and he is shown as prone to violence. *Iscariot* is usually interpreted to mean that the disciple Judas derived from a place called 'Kerioth', which has not been identified. It may, on the other hand, have identified him as one of the *Sicarii*, the Zealot terrorists who resorted to clandestine assassination of Jewish collaborators with the Romans. While overmuch cannot be made of these adopted names, the disciples were possibly not the harmless and vacillating band of visionaries that many Christian theologians would have us believe.

Jesus, while he is shown condemning the other Jewish sects,

48

said nothing about or against the Zealots. If he had done so, the Evangelists would hardly have failed to remark on it. His silence would seem to suggest that he sympathized with their views, and his actions indicate that his objectives were similar, his methods the same.

The Christian evidence shows that Jesus's last visit to Jerusalem came when the Holy City was swollen with excited pilgrims at the time of the Passover, the feast commemorating the miraculous liberation of the Israelites from Egyptian bondage. Jesus's entry into Jerusalem sparked a demonstration which he did not reject, which indeed he invited. He was hailed as the Messiah, the Saviour-King, the heir to David's throne—a proclamation of rebellion which Jesus surely planned deliberately, for he chose to ride upon an ass, in fulfilment of the Messianic prophecy.

The story of the triumphal entry is told in all four Gospels. Luke says that the multitude cried, 'Blessed is the King that Cometh'. Mark records them as shouting, 'Blessed is the Kingdom that Cometh, the Kingdom of Our Father David'. Matthew adds that the mob cried, 'Hosanna to the Son of David'. As it stands, the word 'Hosanna' is meaningless. The more likely cry may have been '*Ossana Barrama*', meaning, 'Free us, Son of David'. Jerome, a Christian writer of the fourth century, found it quoted thus in his version of Matthew's Gospel. The priests say, 'Look the world has gone after him', and the people shout, 'Blessed is the Kingdom that Cometh in the name of the Lord, even the King of Israel'. Matthew says that when Jesus had come into Jerusalem, 'All the city was stirred, saying, "Who is this?" And the people cried: "This is the prophet, Jesus, from Nazareth of Galilee."' The priests and elders did not like it. They feared that the acclamation of a new Messiah-King would lead to another senseless revolt against the Romans. One of them, angry at what was happening, called to Jesus, 'Master, rebuke your followers.' The shouts of joy died away as the crowd silently waited for Jesus's reply. 'I tell you, if these shall hold their peace, even the stones will cry out,' he answered. As the people cheered again, the priests turned away saying, 'We can do nothing, the whole people are following him.'

The implication of political kingship is inescapable, and it is supported by Jesus's further actions.

The 'Cleansing of the Temple', when Jesus overthrew the tables of the money-changers, drove out those who trafficked in sacrificial cattle, and would not allow anyone to carry anything through the Temple, could have occurred only if Jesus and his followers were in control of the Temple courts at the time. This implication is unmistakable, for neither the priests, who controlled the Temple Police, nor the Roman garrison of the Antonia fortress which overlooked the Temple dared arrest him, because they feared the people. The trafficking in the Temple was the perquisite of the High Priests, yet that all-powerful group could do no more than question the authority by which Jesus did these things. In his answer, Jesus challenged *their* authority, telling his listeners the parable of the Wicked Husbandmen, a pointed suggestion, particularly in its concluding words, that Israel would soon have a new master: 'What, therefore, will the lord of the vineyard do? He will come and destroy the husbandmen, and give the vineyard to others.' Perceiving that he spoke against them, the chief priests sought to lay hands on Jesus, but they were afraid of the people. In the Fourth Gospel, these Jewish leaders then gather in council.

'What do we do?' ask the priests. Jesus, they say, has made many signs, and, if he is left alone, the whole nation will believe in him. The Romans will hold the priests responsible, depose them from their authority, and wipe out the Jewish nation. Apparently some members of the council urge that Jesus should be supported. Let us defy the Romans, the hotheads plead. High Priest Caiaphas has other views. 'You know nothing at all. We are too weak to fight the Romans.' It is better, he argues, that one man should die than that the whole nation should perish. Caiaphas prevails and the council orders that any man knowing where Jesus is should reveal it so that he may be arrested. Significantly, the Jewish leaders fear Jesus, not as a religious reformer, but as a political agitator or worse. Their fears may have had greater cause than the Gospels openly reveal.

Jesus's Messianic entry into Jerusalem and his seizure of the Temple appear to have coincided with a Zealot insurrection.

Some such disturbance took place at this time, as the Gospels imply, and it would be extraordinary if the two events were unrelated.

We read in the Gospels of 'murder' being committed, of men being arrested, of the death of eighteen men in the fall of the tower in Siloam, one of the strong-points on the south-eastern city wall. Jesus is told, as the leader who should be informed, of those Galileans (possibly a euphemism for 'Zealots') whose 'blood Pilate had mingled with their sacrifices'—that is, of men who had been slain in the Temple. Jesus advises his informants that if they pursue the same course of action, they too will suffer the same fate. The fate of one particular man, Barabbas, who had been taken prisoner in the 'insurrection', became inseparably bound with that of Jesus.

The insurrection is quelled by Pilate, who, we may assume, demands the arrest of its ringleaders. The *coup* has failed, and Jesus has disappeared. One of his disciples defects and offers to lead the authorities to the secret rendezvous with Jesus, whom he promises to identify. Jesus, meanwhile, has checked that his disciples are armed, though, of course, the carrying of weapons is illegal. When Jesus is shown two swords, presumably by each man, he says, 'It is enough.' The implication is that these swords or knives are concealed within their cloaks, after the manner of the *Sicarii*, the terrorist organization of which Judas *'Iscariot'* may have been a member.

Preparing, perhaps, for flight to Galilee, Jesus and his followers leave the city. They are found at night in the Garden of Gethsemane, on the western slope of the Mount of Olives, by the posse of Temple Police and Roman soldiers. (This armed presence is indicated by the technical terms used in the Fourth Gospel, which identify a cohort and a Tribune.) Judas identifies Jesus by a kiss; the disciples ask, 'Shall we smite with the sword?' and Peter, attempting perhaps to slash his way to freedom, strikes the High Priest's servant, cutting off his right ear, a blow intended to be lethal. Resistance is useless and Jesus orders him to desist; the disciples flee and Jesus is led to the house of the High Priest.

The legal intricacies involved in Jesus's examination by the

Sanhedrin and his trial by Pilate raise questions that are politically important. To the High Priest's question, Jesus unequivocally claims to be the Messiah. The charges are brought by the Jewish authorities, whose duty it was to prosecute in the Procuratorial Court: 'We found this man perverting our nation, forbidding to give tribute to Caesar, and saying he is himself the Messiah, a king.' Jesus makes no answer. To Pilate's question, 'Are you the king of the Jews?' Jesus answers, 'Thou sayest,' or 'You have said it.' He is adjudged guilty, for the Roman law of treason, the *lex Juliana Majestatis* of 48 B.C., made it an offence punishable by death to engage in any activity against the Roman Emperor, without whose consent no king could be proclaimed. Acclamation by the assembled people constituted election contrary to Roman authority. Lack of intent was no defence. The mere appearance of illegal intention was sufficient to prove guilt.

A strange incident occurred at the start of the trial, one for which no entirely satisfactory explanation is possible. Pilate was asked, or he offered, to release either Jesus or Barabbas, who had been taken prisoner 'with them that had made insurrection, men who in the insurrection had committed murder', by which it is meant that they had killed Romans. Barabbas is further described as a 'revolutionary', and he is identified by the word *lestai*, that term employed by the Romans, by Josephus, and by the Gospel writers to describe the Zealots.

These writers employ and may have created the Barabbas incident in order to throw the blame for Jesus's death upon the Jewish leaders. But, assuming Barabbas's existence, our immediate concern is his relationship with Jesus.

His name has been taken by some scholars to provide a clue. Written as two words, 'Bar Abba', it may have described him as the son of a Rabbi. His further name 'Jesus', which the third-century Christian scholar Origen found in a number of ancient codices and which was probably dropped by later scribes as being offensive, suggests a case of mistaken identity. By this theory Pilate is faced with two culprits, both named Jesus, and is uncertain which is the man wanted as the Messiah claimant. His offer to release one or the other was nothing more than an effort to establish identity, which the onlookers cleared up for him. Other scholars find this easy solution to the problem unconvincing. The important point is that the Zealot Barabbas, who had been involved in and may have been the leader of the insurrection at this time, was in some way connected with Jesus, an association which the writers of the Gospels sought to conceal.

Jesus is crucified between two *lestai*, the Roman term for Zealots. They suffer the same 'condemnation' as Jesus and are by their own admission guilty. Above the cross is placed the *titulus* describing the charge on which Jesus had been condemned—THE KING OF THE JEWS. The despair of his followers is expressed by the remark of the disciple Cleophas, 'We hoped it was he who would deliver Israel.' Following Jesus's death and burial his disciples believe that they see him again, whereupon and significantly they inquire, 'Will you at this time restore the kingdom to Israel?' It is a clear indication of their understanding of his mission, and of their devotion to the nationalist cause.

That is the evidence of the Gospels. What does Josephus say? The standard text of his first book, *Concerning the Jewish War*, contains no reference to Jesus, or to the insurrection in which Barabbas was involved. It is a strange omission by an author who blamed both Zealots and Messianists for the later outbreak. Some scholars conclude that *Concerning the Jewish War* in its original form did contain a passage relating to Jesus. Removed later by Christian censors, they believe, it has survived in the Slavonic manuscripts of his book which were found in Russia in 1866. But the authenticity of these manuscripts is doubtful; they are therefore discussed in the Appendix. Whether or not Josephus supplied information about Jesus in his earlier book, he referred to him in his second work, *The Antiquities*. But his original reference was certainly not in the form in which we now read it.

That the passage concerning Jesus is not as Josephus wrote it is attested by Origen. Writing about the year A.D. 250, Origen obviously did not know the passage as it now stands. The Church historian Eusebius, however, who wrote a century after Origen, knew the version we have today. Here lies the proof that the

Christian alteration of the *Antiquities* took place between the years A.D. 250 and 350.

Having read Josephus's book, Origen wrote, 'The wonder is that, though he did not believe our Jesus to be the Christ, he none the less gave witness to so much righteousness in James.' James was Jesus's brother. He had succeeded him as the head of the Messianic movement. Origen remarks that Josephus 'disbelieved in Jesus as the Christ'. His statement reveals that Josephus originally made reference to Jesus and James, and the fact that James is later referred to as 'the brother of Jesus who was called Christ', confirms the existence of an earlier passage about Jesus.

In the *Antiquities* Josephus is referring to the series of tumults in Jerusalem during Pilate's governorship. That section of Josephus's book ends with the words, 'and so sedition was quelled'.

In the traditional version there follows a passage about Jesus:

> Now about this time there arose Jesus, a wise man if indeed he may be called a man. For he was a doer of marvellous acts, a teacher of such men as receive the truth with delight. And he won over to himself many Jews and many also of the Greek nation. He was the Christ. And when, on the indictment of the principal men amongst us, Pilate had sentenced him to the cross, still those who before had loved him did not cease. For he appeared to them on the third day alive again, as the divinely-inspired prophets had told— these and ten thousand other wonderful things concerning him. And until now the race of Christians, so named from him, is not extinct.

But if Josephus had written the passage as it now stands, he must have been a Christian—to which nothing else in his writing or career points. As it reads, it is neither as Josephus wrote it, nor is it entirely a Christian forgery. Origen, to say what he did, must have found a passage in which the Messianic mission of Jesus was definitely repudiated. How the passage may have read originally has been reconstructed by Dr Robert Eisler in *The Messiah Jesus and John the Baptist*. Dr Eisler's restoration of

Josephus's original text is given here in comparison with the standard text to show how easily the Christian misrepresentation could have been effected.

EISLER'S RESTORED TEXT	TRADITIONAL TEXT
Now about this time arose (an occasion for new disturbances) a certain Jesus, a wizard of a man if indeed he may be called a man who was the most monstrous of all men whom his disciples called a son of God, as having done such wonders such as no other man hath ever yet done....	Now about this time arose Jesus a wise man if indeed he may be called a man.
He was in fact a teacher of astonishing tricks to such men as accept the abnormal with delight.	For he was a doer of marvellous acts, a teacher of such men as receive the truth with delight.
And he seduced many Jews and many also of the Greek nation, and was regarded by them as the Messiah.	And he won over to himself many Jews and many also of the Greek nation. He was the Christ.
And when, on the indictment of the principal men among us, Pilate had sentenced him to the cross, still those who before had admired him did not cease to rave. For it seemed to them that having been dead for three days, he had appeared to them alive, as the divinely-inspired prophets had foretold—these and ten thousand other wonderful things concerning him.	And when, on the indictment of the principal men among us, Pilate had sentenced him to the cross, still those who before had loved him did not cease. For he appeared to them on the third day alive again, as the divinely-inspired prophets had told—these and ten thousand other wonderful things—concerning him.
And even now the race of	And until now the race of

| those who are called 'Messianists' after him is not extinct. | Christians, so named from him, is not extinct. |

Josephus's testimony is particularly valuable. It shows that the historian regarded Jesus as a Messianic claimant, which means that there must have been certain aspects of his mission which caused Josephus to view him as an exponent of political Messianism.

Like Zealotism, the movement inspired by Jesus did not die with its founder. Jesus's mission, and his claim to be the Messiah, were not a unique and isolated case, as the Gospels imply, of the rise and fall of a would-be deliverer. The Jews did not expect the Messiah to suffer and die; death invalidated his claim. The case of Jesus was different, for his followers were able to explain his death.

Searching their scriptures they found and applied to Jesus Isaiah's forgotten concept of the Suffering Servant of God. As an apologia it was peculiarly applicable to Jesus's tragic career. 'Behooved it not the Christ [the Messiah] to suffer these things and to enter into his glory?' the disciples preached. Jesus they described as a 'man approved by God' who had been betrayed 'by the determined council and foreknowledge of God', and, having been slain, 'was resurrected by God'. Therefore, 'let all the house of Israel know assuredly that God had made that same Jesus whom ye crucified, both Lord and Christ'.

In other words, Jesus, though dead, was alive and would return to complete his mission. This daring claim gave renewed impetus to the new patriotic movement. Writing of the period in which the Jewish nationalist cause developed, the Roman historian Tacitus remarked that, following the execution of Christus, 'the sect of which he was the founder received a blow which, for a time, checked the growth of a dangerous superstition, but it broke out again and spread with increasing vigour, not only in Judaea, the soil that gave it birth, but even unto the city of Rome'.

As time went by, a number of Jews came to believe that at a moment of national crisis Jesus would reappear leading the Hosts of Heaven.

Six

The Desecration
of the Temple

Following the execution of their leader, the disciples—the men who had fled at Jesus' arrest—went into hiding and met behind closed doors, as is implied in the Fourth Gospel and stated in the Apocryphal *Gospel of Peter*: 'For we were being sought by the authorities as malefactors and as desiring to set fire to the Temple.' This was an allusion to the charge, considered by the Sanhedrin, that Jesus had spoken against the Temple.

Some time following the Crucifixion, possibly only a few days, the disciples left Jerusalem to return to their homes in Galilee, probably mingling on the crowded roads with the returning pilgrims, hoping to remain inconspicuous. They may have feared arrest as associates of the crucified king. In Galilee, they seem to have believed that their dead leader had appeared to them, a remarkable tribute to his forceful personality.

Eventually, and perhaps after some considerable lapse of time, the disciples returned to Jerusalem, where they were not seriously molested. Their advocacy of a dead Messiah probably seemed ridiculous to the Sadducean High Priests, who did not believe in the resurrection of the dead. They contented themselves with admonishing the disciples not to speak in Jesus's name with the intention of 'bringing this man's blood upon us', a reference to the prominent part played by the priestly hierarchy in the arrest and condemnation of Jesus.

On another occasion, when Peter and the other disciples were brought before the Sanhedrin, the divided Council wished to kill them. They are dissuaded by the Pharisee Gamaliel who sceptically advised, 'take care what you do with these men; keep away, for if their plan or undertaking is of men it will fail, but if it is of God, you will not be able to overthrow them'. They might be found opposing God. In his speech, recorded in

Acts, the noted rabbi, known as the 'Glory of the Law', linked Jesus's career with those of other Messianic claimants, and particularly with that of Judas of Galilee. This indicates that Gamaliel considered the movement founded by Jesus to be motivated in a political and revolutionary sense. The Sanhedrin took Gamaliel's advice, ordering the disciples not to speak in the name of Jesus. They were flogged and set at liberty. From the one recorded incident of persecution, the martyrdom of Stephen, the apostles, 'the Fathers of the Church', were exempted. Stephen was stoned by the mob for advocating revolutionary religious change and for desiring to change the Law of Moses. The Fathers, on the other hand, remained faithful to the national religion, worshipping in the Temple, where their new leader became noted for his piety.

The change of leadership is the most remarkable feature of the post-crucifixion period. Peter, whom the Gospels depict as Jesus's principal lieutenant, relinquishes his commanding position to James, the brother of Jesus, who in the Gospels is not even included among Jesus's inner circle. Jesus's whole family had been antagonistic to his mission, but James now becomes undisputed head of the 'Church', beginning a dynastic succession which, after his death, was continued by Jesus's nephew, Symeon. The same system had been adopted by the Zealots.

Meanwhile, in A.D. 37, after Pilate was recalled, Vitelius, the Legate of Syria, came to Jerusalem to conciliate the Jews by remitting certain taxes and by returning to their care the High Priests' vestments. At the same time he reminded them of their servitude by deposing Caiaphas and appointing another High Priest in his place.

On a visit a year later, Vitelius appointed yet another High Priest and, after the death of Tiberius, forced the Jews to swear allegiance to Tiberius's successor, Caligula. This Emperor, by his insane belief in his own divinity, caused a crisis which, except for his sudden death, might have precipitated the revolt of the Jews there and then.

Whether or not he was provoked by the Jews, who had thrown down a Gentile altar at Jamnia, Caligula ordered the new

Legate of Syria, Petronius, to proceed to Jerusalem and set up in the Temple a colossal statue of Jupiter, symbol of the Emperor himself. That Petronius took two legions with him indicates the violent reaction he expected from the Jews against this fundamental threat to their religion. If the Jews refused to admit the statue, Petronius was ordered to put the recalcitrants to death and reduce the whole country to slavery. Petronius moved slowly, hoping perhaps to awe the Jews by his massive preparations to wage war should he be disobeyed. He marched to Ptolemaïs, where he was met by a vast multitude including women and children. They implored him to have regard for their laws, not to force them to transgress and violate their ancestral code. They would rather die, the Jews declared.

To gain time, Petronius informed the Emperor that the construction of a truly magnificent statue could not be hurried. He summoned the Jewish leaders to Tiberias on the shores of Galilee and pointed out that their attitude, in contrast to that of other subject peoples, was an insult to the Emperor. Once again the Jews pleaded that their Law forbade them to place any image not only in their Sanctuary, but anywhere in their country. They cried out that they put their trust in God and were ready to endure everything for the Law.

'Will you then go to war with Rome?' asked Petronius.

'On no account will we fight,' they answered, according to Josephus, 'but we will die sooner than violate our Laws.' Falling on their faces and baring their necks, they defied him to slay them. So stubborn was their determination that they continued their supplications for forty days, neglecting their unsown fields. Their words, records the historian, filled Petronius with astonishment. Unaware that the Jewish prince Agrippa (grandson of Herod) had already in Rome persuaded the Emperor to rescind his order, Petronius wrote to Caligula, explaining the Jews' determination to die, and entreating him not to drive so many thousands to desperation. When he received this letter, the mentally deranged Emperor commanded Petronius to commit suicide. Fortunately, Caligula's letter was delayed in transit. Before it reached him Petronius heard of Caligula's assassination, an event which the Jews accepted as an act of divine intervention.

Josephus admits that the Jews were prepared to go to war; Tacitus states that it actually broke out. The reaction of the Zealots and Christians is ignored by their respective chroniclers. That both sects probably acted violently and in concert, is indicated by the quotation by Mark (XIII) of an oracle, which reflects the attempt by Caligula to violate the Jewish Sanctuary. The allusion would have been clear to any Jew. Mark's reference to the 'abomination of desolation' linked the threat posed in A.D. 39–40 with the desecration of 167 B.C. by the Syrian king Antiochus Epiphanes, who had set up a pagan altar in the Temple. At that time, the Maccabees, the devout priestly family, had fled to the mountains to return with their followers, defeat the Syrians, and set up a Jewish dynasty.

'When you see the abomination of desolation standing where it ought not,' Mark's oracle instructed, 'let them that are in Judaea flee unto the mountains.' They were ordered to abandon their homes and possessions and not to turn back even for a cloak, but to pray that it would not be winter. The oracle stated that, had not God shortened the days, no one would have been saved, 'but God, for the elect's sake, whom he chose, shortened the days', a clear reference to Caligula's sudden death, which the Jews believed had ended the sacrilegious threat.

The term 'the elect' fits both the Zealots and the Christians, those fervid and pious Jews who would have fled into the mountains, in the tradition of the heroic Maccabees, who returned to make war. The inclusion of the Gospel of such a warlike directive suggests, as so much else indicates, a remarkable affinity between the two sects.

Similar strife occurred in Alexandria. Although not directly motivated by Caligula's threat, it had important results for the Jews of the Diaspora. When he became Emperor, Caligula had appointed Agrippa King of Trachonitis and Gaulanitis, the territories east of Jordan. On his way from Rome to Palestine, Agrippa visited Alexandria where he was greeted by the Jews with great pomp, befitting a Jewish king. Their vociferous welcome infuriated the Greek citizens, who staged a mock procession, dressing up the local idiot and hailing him with cries of '*Marin*', the Aramaic word for 'Our Lord'. This parody of Jewish kingship caused riots in which the Jews were plundered, tortured, and killed.

The Roman Prefect, Flaccus, did nothing to restrain this flare-up of anti-Semitism. Fearing the Emperor's wrath, the Gentiles demanded the erection of Caligula's statue in the synagogues. Both camps sent embassies to Rome to lay their grievances before the Emperor. But Caligula's successor, Claudius, issued a Decree—the Charter of Jewish Liberties, as it has been called. This granted that 'the Jews throughout the Empire are to be allowed to keep their ancestral customs without let or hindrance'. But they were warned to use the Emperor's kindness with moderation and 'not to act contemptuously towards the superstitions of other races'.

Claudius extended his conciliatory policy to Palestine and in A.D. 41 granted rule of most of Palestine to Agrippa, a man of great ability. His piety and devotion to Judaism were recognized by the Jews, who welcomed him as a ruler with the title of Herod Agrippa I. He was half-Jewish, a grandson of Herod the Great, and a descendant, through his grandmother, of the Maccabean kings. The Tetrarch Antipas was banished and Judaea and Galilee were reunited. The hated tribute became merely a tax paid for the upkeep of a Jewish king who appointed the High Priest; the priestly vestments remained in Jewish control. No longer could the Jews complain that they were ruled by pagan foreigners. Agrippa was the ideal ruler to bridge the chasm between the Romans and the Jews.

The Zealot reaction to the return of Jewish rule is unrecorded, and the Christian is obscured by Luke, the author of *Acts*, who apparently had something dangerous to conceal. Luke accuses Herod Agrippa of persecuting the Church. 'And he killed James, the brother of John with the sword'—a form of execution for political crime. (For a religious crime he would have been stoned to death.) And when Agrippa saw that his execution pleased the Jews he proceeded to seize Peter also. Peter, however, escapes from prison, and goes to 'another place'.

Peter disappears from the narrative of *Acts*. Luke, Paul's companion and friend, now concentrates on his hero's missionary activities. Paul travels through the cities of Asia Minor to Corinth in Greece, where he is accused of being 'one of those subverters of civilization, men who are actively opposed to the Imperial Decrees, saying that there is another king, one Jesus'. Paul sought to escape this charge by declaring that he 'was pure from the blood of all men'. He was saying that he was not a political revolutionary.

Paul had not known Jesus; he claimed to have been converted by a vision. He rejected the concept of Jesus as a Jewish Messiah; Paul saw him as the World Saviour. Paul's beliefs and teaching brought him into conflict with the Fathers of the Church, the men who had known Jesus. According to Luke, the differences are minor and easily settled, and Paul carries the new faith triumphantly to Rome. It is a false picture. Paul's own letters, written forty years before Acts, reveal the truth.

Paul came to Jerusalem about A.D. 55 to seek support for his unique interpretation of Jesus's nature and mission. He was forced to bow to the unchallengeable authority of the Church Fathers. He admitted defeat, ceding victory to his powerful opponents.

They invited him to perform a ritual test in the Temple to prove his Jewish orthodoxy. It was an astute move, for his submission would shatter his prestige with his Gentile converts. Placed in a fatal dilemma, he brought Gentiles into the National Shrine. That constituted a capital crime. 'No stranger,' stated the warning inscription, 'is to enter.' Written in Hebrew, Latin and Greek, it declared, 'Whoever is caught will be responsible for his own death, which will ensue.'

Paul was detected and attacked by the mob. Rescued by the Roman guards, he was accused by the Temple authorities before the Procurator Felix of violating the national religion. He claimed Roman citizenship by reason of his birth at Tarsus in Cilicia, and right of appeal to Caesar. Felix's successor, Festus, sent Paul to Rome for trial. Luke does not record his fate.

Paul's special interpretation of the faith, his missionary activities, and his dispute with the leaders of the Messianic movement had no influence on the events which led to the outbreak of the Jewish revolt. But the Christian squabble had far-reaching consequences. Its strange reversal requires detailed discussion when the siege and fall of Jerusalem are assessed in the final chapter.

Tragically for the Jews, Agrippa's reign was cut short. He died in A.D. 44 soon after he had started to build a 'Third Wall' to the north of Jerusalem, to surround the new suburb of Bezetha. Had it been completed 'it would have rendered ineffectual all the efforts of the Romans in the subsequent siege', remarks Josephus with his usual exaggeration. Agrippa's intention to strengthen the city's defence resulted in the suspicion that he was preparing to defy the Romans, and he was told to desist, an order he dared not disobey.

His seventeen-year-old son, also named Agrippa, was considered too young to succeed him. The rapacious Procurators returned to Palestine to rule the Jews as the representatives of a pagan Emperor. With the advantage of hindsight, Josephus detected the sense of doom and of impending catastrophe which beset the Jews, many of whom, however, were buoyed up by the belief that God would intervene to deliver them from Roman rule.

Seven

The Procurators
Return

The return of direct Roman rule incited the Jews, once again, to resist the desecration of their Holy Land. Soon after his arrival in A.D. 44 Cuspius Fadus, the first of the new Procurators, was forced to clear Judaea of 'brigands' and 'robber bands', says Josephus. The historian employed his usual derogatory terms to describe the revolutionaries and Zealots. The 'arch-brigand' Tholomaeus, 'who had inflicted severe mischief', was brought in chains to Fadus, who put him to death. At this time —though Josephus does not say whether it caused Tholomaeus's rebellion or was its result—Fadus, reversing the decree which had operated since A.D. 37, confiscated the vestments of the High Priest, 'who did not gainsay him'. The Legate of Syria, Cassius Longinus, arrived in Jerusalem with a large force, 'out of fear that Fadus's commands would force the Jewish people to rebellion'. The Romans were fully aware of the intransigence of their Judaean subjects and of Jewish determination to oppose Roman rule.

Overawed, perhaps, by Longinus's legions, the Jews meekly petitioned to send a delegation to the Emperor for permission to retain the sacred robe. On being told that it would be granted if they delivered up the delegates' children as hostages, they promptly agreed. This Roman demand suggests that they feared trouble while the Jewish leaders were abroad. On the arrival of these envoys in Rome, Claudius, who listened to the entreaties of the young Agrippa on their behalf, granted their request. He instructed Fadus to return the robe to Jewish custody. He went further, according the right of appointment of the High Priest to the late King Agrippa's brother—Herod, King of Chalcis—and to his successors.

Claudius's conciliatory policy and his reversal of Fadus's un-

popular order failed to stem Jewish unrest. It may have served
to encourage it, for the Jews were ever ready to accept Roman
actions in their favour as marks of that divine providence
which, they believed, would protect them from the severity of
foreign rule and ultimately free them. Eager as some Jews may
have been to co-operate with the Romans, others were not so
inclined. We read in Josephus that a certain impostor—or
magician, as he calls him—named Theudas,

> persuaded the majority of the people to take up their pos-
> sessions and follow him to the Jordan river. He stated that
> he was a prophet and that at his command the river would
> be parted and would provide them with an easy passage.
> With this talk he deceived many. Fadus did not permit
> them to reap the fruit of their folly, but sent a squadron
> of cavalry. These fell upon them unexpectedly, slew many
> of them and took many prisoners. Theudas himself was
> captured, whereupon they cut off his head and brought it
> to Jerusalem.

Theudas is also mentioned in the *Acts*, where he is linked
by the learned Pharisee Gamaliel with the other Messianic
claimants, Judas and Jesus, both men of Galilee. Theudas
appears to have been a religious fanatic believing himself
another Moses who would lead his people on another exodus
into the desert in order to escape heathen rule. That he and
his peaceful followers were intercepted and slain suggests that
the Romans were either suspicious of his intentions or un-
necessarily severe. Theudas's rising, if such it can be called,
occurred in A.D. 44-45, the last year of Fadus's governorship.

Claudius next appointed as Procurator Tiberius Alexander,
an apostate Jew, member of a distinguished Alexandrian
family. The Emperor's good intention was clear, for the new
Procurator might be expected to understand the Jews as no
Roman could. Josephus said that Tiberius Alexander 'by ab-
staining from all interference with the customs of the country
kept all the nation at peace'. In the *Antiquities* Josephus
qualifies this happy state of affairs. Whether the trouble was

provoked by the great famine that struck Judaea at this time or by some unrecorded act of the Procurator, Tiberius Alexander crucified James and Simon, the sons of Judas of Galilee. What they had done is not stated; it is most likely that they had led a Zealot rising. Their execution suggests that the mature sons of the founder of Zealotism had kept the movement alive as the spearhead of Jewish resistance. Another son of Judas, Menahem, succeeded to the leadership.

The Romans seem to have been equally suspicious of the Christians. That the story of Jesus's alleged resurrection was well known to the Romans is claimed by Professor A. Momigliano (*L'Opera dell'Imperatore Claudio*). He cites the Latin inscription found at Nazareth in 1870. This 'Ordinance of Caesar', as it is headed, he dates by internal evidence to the reign of the Emperor Claudius (A.D. 41–54). Other scholars dispute this dating on the ground that the reference to 'Caesar', without further identification, indicates the Emperor Augustus, who died in A.D. 14. The English translation of the *Edict* is published by M. P. Charlesworth (*Documents Illustrating the Reigns of Claudius and Nero*), and reads:

> It is my pleasure that graves and tombs remain undisturbed in perpetuity for those who have made them for the cult of their ancestors or children or members of their house. If however any man lay information that another has either demolished them or has in any way extracted the buried or has maliciously transferred them to other places in order to wrong them, or has displaced the sealing or other stones, against such a one I order that a trial be instituted, as in respect of the gods, so in regard to the cult of mortals. For it shall be much more obligatory to honour the buried. Let it be absolutely forbidden for anyone to destroy them. In case of contravention I desire that the offender be sentenced to capital punishment on charge of violation of sepulchre.

If Professor Momigliano is correct in his identification, the *Edict* indicates Roman endeavour to prevent the recurrence of the act of violation of sepulchre which they thought had given impetus to the spread of a 'dangerous superstition'.

Returning to more reliable evidence, we learn from Josephus that the arrival of the next Procurator, Ventilius Cumanus, led to an uprising in Jerusalem in which many people lost their lives. The fanatical rage of the Jews saw in the rude act of a Roman soldier not an insult to themselves but a blasphemy against God. The usual crowd, states the historian, had assembled for the Passover, and the Roman cohort stationed in the Antonia fortress had taken up its position on the portico overlooking the Temple, as was the practice on Feast-days to prevent disorders arising from such a concourse of people. On the fourth day of the festival, 'one of the soldiers uncovered his genitals and exhibited them to the multitude'. In the *Antiquities*, Josephus says that the soldier 'raising his robe, stooped in an indecent attitude, so as to turn his backside to the Jews, and made a noise in keeping with his posture'.

Whatever the nature of the soldier's offence, some of the more hotheaded young men and 'seditious persons' in the crowd started to fight, picking up stones and hurling them at the soldiers. The bolder ones reviled Cumanus, asserting that he had prompted the soldier's action. Cumanus, not a little provoked at the insulting remarks, merely admonished the people to 'put an end to this lust for revolution', and not set disorders ablaze during the festival. Fearing a general attack, he called up reinforcements. Upon their arrival, the soldiers rushed into the porticos (at the sides of the Temple court). The Jews were seized with irresistible panic and turned to flee, 'but, since the exits were narrow they, supposing that they were being pursued, pushed together in their flight and crushed to death many of their number who were caught in the narrow passage'. In one account Josephus estimated the casualties at 30,000 and in another at 20,000, both obviously wild exaggerations. 'Such were the calamities produced by the indecent behaviour of a single soldier,' Josephus sanctimoniously observes.

This calamity was followed by other disorders, originating with 'brigands', or 'seditious revolutionaries', who waylaid a servant of Caesar and robbed him of all his belongings. When Cumanus heard of this outrage, he sent a punitive expedition to plunder the neighbouring villages and bring before him in fetters their most eminent citizens, whom he reprimanded for not having pursued and arrested the robbers. A soldier, finding in one village a copy of the sacred Law, tore it in pieces and flung it into the fire, at the same time uttering blasphemies. 'At that,' states Josephus, 'the Jews were roused as though it were their whole country which had been consumed in the flames.' Collecting in large numbers, they hurried to Caesarea and implored Cumanus not to leave unpunished the author of such an outrage against God. They could not endure living, they declared, when their ancestral code had been thus wantonly insulted. Alarmed by the thought of a fresh revolution, Cumanus ordered the soldier to be led through the ranks of his accusers, whereupon he was beheaded.

An even more serious disturbance occurred when a number of Galilean pilgrims, passing through Samaria on their way to attend a festival in Jerusalem, were attacked; some were killed. Hearing of their murder, other Galileans assembled with the intention of making war on the Samaritans. Messengers sent ahead to Jerusalem aroused the masses, who, abandoning the festival, took up arms and dashed off to Samaria, ignoring the entreaties of the magistrates to desist. The Jews invited the assistance of men whom Josephus, as usual, calls 'brigands'. These 'rioters', he says, under the leadership of Eleazar, the son of Deinaeus, whom he calls a Zealot and who, he says, 'for many years lived in the mountains'—together with another man named Alexander burned and sacked certain Samaritan villages, massacring the inhabitants without distinction of age.

Cumanus, who had previously refused to intervene, marched to the afflicted area and in an encounter with the insurgent Jews slew a large number and took prisoners, including many of Eleazar's companions. Eleazar himself escaped—to ravage the countryside for another ten years or so before he was captured and executed by the Procurator Antonius Felix. In the *Talmud* Eleazar is described as a leader who tried to force the Messianic redemption of Israel before God's chosen time.

The magistrates of Jerusalem, dressed in sackcloth and ashes, had followed their people, imploring them to return home before bringing Roman wrath upon Jerusalem. Yielding to these entreaties, most of the Jews dispersed, but, states Josephus, many, emboldened by impunity, 'had recourse to robbery'. Insurrections, fostered by the most reckless, broke out all over the country. The Zealots, Josephus says, returned to their strongholds—a term which suggests that they had been waging guerilla war against the Romans for a considerable time.

The leaders of the Samaritans, for their part, sought redress from the Legate of Syria, Quadratus, who also heard the Jewish complaint that it was the Samaritans, by their murder of the pilgrims, who had started the disturbance. Cumanus refused to take proceedings against the murderers. He had been bribed by the Samaritans, the Jews declared. Deferring judgment, Quadratus travelled to Samaria, where a full hearing convinced him that the Samaritans had been responsible for the disorder. He crucified both the Samaritans and the rebellious Jews whom Cumanus had taken prisoner.

At a second hearing, Quadratus was told that a leader of the Jews named Doetus, together with four other revolutionaries, had instigated the mob to revolt against the Romans. These, with fourteen others, were executed.

The Samaritan leaders, together with the Jewish High Priests, Jonathan and Ananias, the latter's son Ananus, the Captain of the Temple, Cumanus the Procurator, and the Tribune Celer, were all sent in chains to Rome for the Imperial courts to make a decision. (The Syrian Legate, fearing a revolution, visited Jerusalem, where he found the people peacefully celebrating the Passover.) Claudius, who heard the case himself, on discovering that the Samaritans had been the first to stir up trouble, ordered those brought before him to be put to death. He condemned Cumanus to exile and ordered Celer to be returned to Jerusalem, dragged round the city in public spectacle, and then beheaded.

Once again the Emperor of Rome had been lenient to his Jewish subjects. That Claudius chose to humble his Procurator and send his Tribune to a barbarous death to please the Jews indicates the extent to which he was prepared to go in conciliation. Such incidents indicate the growth of patriotic resistance led by the Zealots. They were not alone in their opposition to Roman rule. Josephus attributed the blame for the catastrophe that befell his people in the final revolt both to these 'brigands' and to the men whom he calls 'impostors' and 'deceivers'. He probably meant those who taught the triumphant return of their Messiah, and the imminent coming of the Kingdom of Heaven.

The Christian Messianists caused trouble not only in Rome but perhaps also in Alexandria. Suetonius states that in A.D. 49 Claudius 'expelled from Rome the Jews who made constant disturbances at the instigation of Christus'. His statement is confirmed by Luke, who says that 'Claudius had decreed that all the Jews should leave Rome.' Two of the expelled Christians, Aquila and his wife, Priscilla, went to Corinth (Greece), where they encountered Paul (*Acts* 18). Dio Cassius states that Claudius closed the synagogues in Rome to prevent seditious discussion, but allowed the Jews otherwise to continue their traditional mode of life. The inference that the Christians were the root of the trouble in Alexandria is less certain. Claudius wrote to its citizens warning them not to entertain Jews from Syria (of which Palestine was a small province) if they did not wish to be considered abettors of a 'pest which threatens the whole world'.

The Christian Messianists were now carrying their political message far beyond Palestine, preaching to the Jewish Diaspora that Jesus would return to complete his mission. The Emperor of Rome considered such propaganda subversive, even a 'pest' which threatened his Empire. That the Christians sent emissaries abroad to stir up trouble is also implied by Tacitus. Purely religious teachings alone could hardly have caused such dissension, for the Christians were orthodox Jews whose reverence for Judaism was no less than that of their co-religionists.

As his reign progressed, the Emperor Claudius, according to Professor Momigliano, adopted a harsher attitude towards the Jews. This may have been induced by the subversive activities of the Christians. The Roman attitude became progressively more severe during the reign of Claudius's successor Nero, who accused the Christians of burning Rome.

Eight

The Rising Tide
Against the Romans

In A.D. 48 Claudius gave the rule of Galilee, as well as of the territory ruled by his uncle, Philip, to the young Agrippa (later Agrippa II) and sent Antonius Felix to govern Judaea. Soon after his arrival, Felix scandalized the Jews by seducing Agrippa's married sister, Drusilla, then marrying her contrary to the laws of her ancestors.

In Judaea, states Josephus, 'things were constantly going from bad to worse', for 'the country was again infested with bands of brigands and impostors who deceived the people.' Not a day passed in which Felix did not capture and put to death many of them. Inducing him to surrender by pledging no harm would befall him, Felix captured Eleazar, son of Deinaeus, 'who had organized a band of brigands', and many of his associates. Felix sent them to Rome for trial, the result of which is unrecorded. Others he crucified, as well as those of the common people who had been convicted of complicity in their crimes. Their number, says Josephus, was 'incalculable'.

But, 'while the country was thus cleared of these pests,' he goes on, 'a new species of banditti was springing up in Jerusalem, the so-called *Sicarii*, who committed murder in broad daylight in the heart of the city.' The festivals were their special seasons, when they would mingle with the crowd, carrying under their clothing short daggers with which they stabbed their enemies unnoticed. When the victims fell, the murderers joined in the cries of indignation and, through this plausible behaviour, were never discovered.

Josephus adopted the Roman name, derived from the Latin *sica*—curved knife—to describe these terrorists. As we have seen, Judas 'Iscariot' may have been one of them.

The *Sicarii's* first victim was Jonathan, the High Priest, for whose death Josephus gives, in *Antiquities*, a remarkable and dubious explanation. This passage reads like the garbled version of gossip heard after a considerable lapse of time and set down verbatim. It apparently suited the historian's apologetic purpose to represent these *Sicarii* as assassins who would kill for money.

According to Josephus's informant, Felix bribed Jonathan's most trusted friend to hire the *Sicarii* to murder the High Priest. Felix bore a grudge against Jonathan because of his frequent admonitions to improve his administration.

Jonathan's assassination remained unpunished, and from that time forth, states Josephus, 'the brigands with perfect impunity used to go to the city during festivals, with their weapons concealed, and mingle with the crowds'. In this way, he claims 'they slew some because they were private enemies, and others because they were paid to do so by someone else'. The *Sicarii* committed their murders even in the Temple itself.

The panic caused by the *Sicarii* was more alarming than the calamity itself, for everyone, as on a battlefield, hourly expected death. Men kept watch on their enemies and even distrusted their friends. Yet, even when their suspicions had been aroused and they were on their guard, they fell, so swift were the conspirators, and so crafty were they in eluding detection.

Josephus's later references to these *Sicarii* indicate that they were a branch of the Zealots, for he says that, 'With such pollution the deeds of these *lestai* (Zealots) infect the city.' Others, he says, were equally guilty:

> Besides these there arose another body of villains, with purer hands but more impious intentions, who no less than the assassins ruined the peace of the city. Deceivers and impostors, under pretence of divine inspiration fostering revolutionary changes, they persuaded the mob to act like madmen, and led them out into the desert under the belief that God would there give them tokens of deliverance.

Many, he says, were persuaded and paid the penalty for their folly, for 'against them Felix, regarding this as but the preliminary to insurrection, sent a body of cavalry and heavily armed infantry, and put a large number to the sword'.

While it is possible that these so-called impostors and deceivers were harmless religious fanatics, it is more probable that by these scornful terms Josephus identified the Christian Messianists. These 'deceivers', with 'divine inspiration', spoke of the imminence of the coming Kingdom and the return of their crucified Messiah; no other known group fits this description so well. The Romans, too, included the Christians among those whom they believed had fomented and instigated the great revolt of the Jews.

Continuing with his story, Josephus reports that a 'still worse blow was dealt the Jews by the Egyptian false prophet'—a well-known charlatan. Unnamed, he is mentioned in *Acts* (21:38) as leading '4,000 *Sicarii*', which indicates that he was a Zealot. This man, for whom Paul was mistaken in the Temple by those Jews who wished to kill him, collected a large following of dupes. He led about 30,000 (says Josephus with his usual exaggeration) by a circuitous route to the Mount of Olives, where he asserted that at his command the walls of Jerusalem would fall down and provide them with an entrance into the city, enabling them to overpower the Roman garrison. Forewarned of this attack, Felix met the insurgents, slaying four hundred and taking two hundred prisoners. The Egyptian escaped and disappeared.

No sooner, Josephus continues, were these disorders reduced than the inflammation broke out again in another quarter. Banding together, the 'impostors' and 'brigands' incited many people to revolt, exhorting them to exert their independence and threatening to kill any who submitted to Roman domination. Groups of these men looted the houses of the wealthy, murdered their owners, and set villages on fire. 'The effect of their frenzy was thus felt throughout all Judaea, and every day saw the war fanned into fiercer flame,' Josephus remarks.

Josephus reports the co-operation of 'brigands' and 'impostors' (his standard terms for 'wonder-workers' or 'magicians', the

73

popular names for Messianic pretenders) and the patriotic Zealots. He relates that they banded in military companies, for the purpose of terrorizing the fainthearted, killing the wealthy who collaborated with the Romans, and inciting revolt.

Another disturbance broke out in Caesarea, the city where Jews and Gentiles had long been in dispute over their respective civil rights. In A.D. 59–60, both sides took up arms and were quietened only when the Procurator Felix sent the notables of each party to Rome to discuss their problems with the Emperor. Felix himself was recalled to Rome to answer their accusations.

At this time, too, a quarrel developed in Jerusalem between the High Priests and the lesser priests. Josephus is suspiciously silent about the reason. Behind it may have lain the attitudes of each group to Roman-Jewish relations. When King Agrippa bestowed the High Priesthood upon Ishmael, the son of Phabi, Josephus says, 'there was enkindled mutual enmity and class-warfare'. Each faction recruited bands of 'reckless revolutionaries'. When they clashed there was no one to rebuke them, since no one seemed to be in charge of the city. 'Such was the shamelessness and effrontery which possessed the High-Priests, they were actually so brazen as to send slaves to the threshing-floors to receive the tithes that were due to the priests, that the poorer priests starved to death.'

Two years later the High Priest Ananias again seized the tithes and the poorer priests starved once more. On this occasion Josephus is far less condemnatory, for, while he identifies the chief priests as the guilty party, he praises Ananias, who 'daily advanced his reputation and was splendidly rewarded by the goodwill and esteem of the citizens'.

A certain restlessness respecting religious ceremonial can be detected amongst the lower clergy about this time. During King Agrippa I's reign certain Levites had been granted the right to sing hymns as well as chant psalms, an innovation which shocked the Pharisees. The Levites also demanded the right to wear linen, like the ordinary priests. It is improbable that the cause of the quarrel was religious, for the repercussions of such an unusual event would not have been easily forgotten.

This priestly quarrel may have been due to the patriotism

74

of the lesser priests who at the start of the revolt joined the revolutionaries. By devious reporting Josephus may have hoped to obscure the unpalatable fact that these priests had risen against the Roman collaborating aristocracy. If this be the true explanation, Jewish resistance had now developed into a national movement, not one inspired solely by fanatical impostors and lawless brigands, as Josephus preferred to assert.

The Procurator Felix was succeeded by Porcius Festus, who proceeded to attack 'the principal plague of the country'. When he arrived he found that 'Judaea was being devastated by bandits' who plundered and set fire to the villages, one by one. The *Sicarii* and the Zealots were particularly active. Josephus relates that Festus sent a force of cavalry and infantry 'against the dupes of a certain impostor who had promised them salvation and rest from troubles, if they chose to follow him into the wilderness'. The soldiers destroyed both the deceiver and those who had followed him.

Josephus thus records yet another Zealot rising under an unnamed Messianic leader who promised salvation. That leader's fate, however, did not deter others from championing the nationalistic cause.

Although the next incident has nothing to do with revolutionary activities, it provides an insight into Roman-Jewish relations at governmental level. King Agrippa II had built in his palace at Jerusalem a room that overlooked the Temple, which enabled him and his guests to 'spy' upon the proceedings and sacrifices within the Temple. This annoyed the eminent men of the city, who erected a high wall to block the royal view. At the same time they increased the height of the Temple's western portico in order to shut out the sight of the Roman guards, who were posted at festivals to supervise the proceedings, as we have seen. Both parties to the dispute sent deputations to Nero. Prompted by the Empress Poppaea, the Emperor decided in favour of the priests, condoning their action. Agrippa deposed the High Priest and appointed in his place Joseph Kabi.

Kabi's appointment was short-lived. During the interregnum between the death of Festus and the arrival of his successor, Lucceius Albinus, Agrippa dismissed him and bestowed the office upon Ananus, son of a former High Priest, another Ananus, whose five sons all became High Priests. Josephus described the younger Ananus as rash in temper and of unusual daring. Seizing the favourable opportunity provided by the absence of the Procurator, Ananus convened the Sanhedrin in A.D. 62. He accused of transgressing the law the man whom Josephus identifies as 'James, the brother of Jesus, who was called the Christ [Messiah].' Together with others James was delivered to the crowd to be stoned to death.

The leader of the Christians was accused and put to death over the protests of men whom Josephus describes as 'those who were considered the most fair-minded and who were in strict observance of the Law'. These were the Pharisees, some of whom begged Agrippa II to restrain Ananus. Others hurried to meet the new Procurator Albinus. They claimed that Ananus had no authority to convene the Sanhedrin without the Procurator's consent. Albinus wrote to Ananus threatening vengeance, and Agrippa II deposed the High Priest from the office he had held for only three months.

While Josephus neglects to state the charges made against James, he implies that they were unjust. The vagueness of his narrative suggests that he preferred to conceal the reason for James's sudden unpopularity with the Sadducean aristocracy. A different version of James's death was supplied a hundred years later by the Christian writer Hegessipus, who may have derived his confused story from Christian tradition. Freed from its obvious absurdities, his account relates that when James testified that Jesus was the Saviour, 'there arose a tumult among the Jews, Pharisees and Scribes, saying that there was a danger that the Jews would expect Jesus as the Messiah'. In this version of the story James is thrown from the Pinnacle of the Temple, its south-eastern corner, and is despatched by a club.

No satisfactory explanation for James's execution can be advanced. He appears to have been a respected member of the Jewish community worshipping in the Temple, and neither feared nor disliked by the Pharisees—indications that he had not advocated revolutionary religious changes. Yet his alleged offence was apparently religious, since he was stoned to death.

A clue may lie in the earlier statement by the author of *Acts* (6:7) that many priests had joined the Christian movement. Perhaps James became embroiled in the dispute among the priests.

Whatever the nature of James's offence, another disturber of the peace came off better, as Josephus relates. One Jesus, the son of a rude peasant, came to Jerusalem to attend the Feast of the Tabernacles. He suddenly began to cry out,

> A voice from the east, a voice from the west, a voice from the four winds; a voice against Jerusalem and the Sanctuary, a voice against the bridegroom and the bride, a voice against all the people.
>
> Day and night he went about all the alleys with this cry on his lips. Some of the leading citizens, incensed at these ill-omened words, arrested the fellow and severely chastised him. But he, without a word on his own behalf or for the private ear of those who smote him, only continued his cries as before. Thereupon the magistrates, supposing, as was indeed the case, that the man was under some supernatural impulse, brought him before the Roman governor [Albinus, called Albinius by Josephus]; there, although flayed to the bone with scourges, he neither sued for mercy nor shed a tear, but, merely introducing the most mournful of variations into his ejaculation, responded to each stroke with, 'Woe to Jerusalem!' When Albinius, the governor, asked him who and whence he was and why he uttered these cries, he answered him never a word, but unceasingly reiterated his dirge over the city, until Albinius pronounced him a maniac and let him go. During the whole period up to the outbreak of war he neither approached nor was seen talking to any of the citizens, but daily, like a prayer that he had conned, repeated his lament, 'Woe to Jerusalem!' He neither cursed any of them who beat him from day to day, nor blessed those who offered him food; to all men that melancholy presage was his one reply. His cries were loudest at the festivals. So for seven years and five months he continued his wail, his voice never

flagging, nor his strength exhausted, until in the siege, having seen his presage avenged, he found rest.

Reverting to his story of the events which led to his people's clash with Rome, Josephus records that 'there was no form of villainy that he [Albinus] omitted to practice'. The historian, who has hitherto blamed the extremists for the worsening of Roman-Jewish relations, is now opening his defence for his people, who, he claims, were provoked to revolt by the atrocious behaviour of both Albinus and Gessius Florus, who succeeded him in A.D. 64. This position is supported by Tacitus, no lover of the Jews. He states that they were provoked beyond endurance, and that the anger of the Romans was aggravated because the Jews alone had not given way to them.

In accusing Albinus Josephus says, 'Not only did he, in his official capacity, steal and plunder private property and burden the whole nation with extraordinary taxes, but he accepted ransoms from relatives of those who had been imprisoned for robbery by the local councils or by former Procurators.' The only malefactors who remained in prison were those who failed to pay the price of freedom. This general release from jail stimulated the audacity of the revolutionary party. Josephus depicts each ruffian—surrounded by his own band of followers over whom he towered like a 'brigand-chief'—employing his bodyguard to plunder peaceful citizens. So fearful were the victims that they kept their grievances to themselves, or cringed to the wretches for fear of punishment. No one, states Josephus, dared to speak his mind. 'From this date,' he laments, 'were sown in the city the seeds of its impending doom.'

The *Sicarii*, most of whom Albinus had exterminated soon after his arrival in Judaea but who now enjoyed a revival, entered Jerusalem at night and kidnapped the Secretary of Eleazar, the Captain of the Temple, and the son of the High Priest Ananias. The secretary was held as hostage to secure the release of ten of their men. Even greater troubles followed. Emboldened by success, the *Sicarii* kidnapped members of the High Priest's own staff, thus securing the exchange of more members of their group.

Learning that he would soon be superseded, and desiring to gain some reputation for service to the people he had ruled, Albinus executed the remaining prisoners who had been sentenced to death. He released those who had been cast into prison for trifling offences, whereupon, states Josephus, the land was again 'infested with brigands'.

It must have been about this time that Josephus travelled to Rome to intercede on behalf of certain priests, and he may not have been living in Jerusalem at the time of the arrival of the new Procurator, Florus, in A.D. 64. By the end of the year, however, Josephus was in Jerusalem, perhaps now convinced by his journey of the power of Rome and the folly of Jewish resistance.

It is hard to believe Josephus's account of Florus's barbarous behaviour. According to Josephus, he set out to provoke the Jews into revolt in order to conceal his own crimes, and to prevent them from denouncing him to the Emperor. Florus's behaviour made his predecessor appear a paragon of virtue, and caused the Jews to praise Albinus as a benefactor who had at least tried to conceal his villainy. Florus, on the other hand, flaunted his wickedness, omitting no form of pillage or unjust treatment, so that, says Josephus, 'we prepared to perish together rather than by degrees'.

The Romans, possibly exasperated by Jewish resistance, reacted with increased severity. Now the Emperor Nero, to whom the Gentiles and Jews of Caesarea had appealed, decided in favour of the former. To celebrate their victory the Gentiles offered a sacrifice outside the chief Jewish synagogue. Florus refused to intervene and fanned Jewish anger even further by taking seventeen talents from the Temple treasury, which he claimed was due in tribute. The Jews' response has a modern ring: certain young malcontents paraded through the city carrying baskets, begging contributions for the 'unfortunate destitute'—a barbed jest which infuriated Florus. Marching to Jerusalem, he ordered the leading citizens to meet him on the city's outskirts. Anxious to forestall the Procurator's wrath, they greeted him obsequiously, whereupon he ordered his cavalry to ride them down. Entering the city, Florus delivered it for plunder and massacre to his soldiers, who entered the houses,

79

slaughtering their inhabitants. In the panic that ensued, many were killed. Others were brought before Florus, who ordered them to be scourged and crucified. Those who claimed Roman citizenship were not exempted. Florus even insulted the Princess Bernice, Agrippa II's sister, forcing her to watch the torture and execution of his victims.

These atrocities occurred on June 3, A.D. 66. Though the High Priests succeeded in soothing the multitude, they exasperated the 'factious party'. Another clash developed between the Romans and the Jews outside the city, when the soldiers clubbed and trampled the peaceful protestors. Josephus vividly describes the terrible scene, which he may have witnessed:

> Many fell beneath the blows of the Romans, a still larger number under the pressure of their own companions. Around the gates the crush was terrible. As each strove to pass in first, the flight of all was retarded, and dreadful was the fate of any who stumbled; suffocated and mangled by the crowds that trod them down, they were obliterated and their bodies so disfigured that their relatives could not recognize them to give them burial. The troops pushed in with the fugitives, mercilessly striking anyone who fell into their hands, and so thrust the crowd back through the quarter called Bezetha, trying to force their way through and occupy the temple and the castle of Antonia. Florus, with the same object in view, led his men out from the court of the palace and struggled to reach the fortress. But he was foiled in this purpose; for he found himself faced by the people, who turned upon him and checked his advance, while others, posting themselves along the roofs, kept the Romans under continuous fire. Overwhelmed by the missiles from above and incapable of cutting their way through the crowds that blocked the narrow alleys, the soldiers beat a retreat to their camp adjoining the palace.

Goaded to fury by Florus's insane acts, the Jews turned on their oppressors. To prevent Florus from seizing the Temple, the revolutionaries broke down the porticos connecting it to the Antonia fortress, whereupon Florus quit the city, leaving a cohort to guard the Antonia and the royal palace. The Jewish leaders appealed to Cestius Gallus, the Legate of Syria. He sent the Tribune Neapolitanius to investigate. Significantly, Neapolitanius went unguarded on his tour of the city to satisfy himself of the temper of the people. He commended them for their loyalty to Rome. The citizens appealed also to Agrippa II, who had returned to Jerusalem, asking him to send an embassy to Rome to denounce Florus, for they feared that the Jews might come under suspicion of revolt after so dreadful a massacre.

Agrippa II then made a long speech which probably represented Josephus's views. (Authors of this time tended to put their own words into the mouth of someone else.) Agrippa warned the Jews of the dangers of war against the Romans, who had conquered the Greeks, Gauls, Spaniards, Germans, the peoples of Asia, and even the British, though they were protected by the ocean. (This was possibly the first historical reference to Britain's sea-girt isolation.) He warned them also that they would find no allies. Pay your tribute and restore the porticos, he advised. Thus far, the people had listened to their King in respectful silence. But when he tried to persuade them to submit to Florus, they became exasperated, heaping abuse upon him. Some even took up stones to throw at the King. Seeing that the passions of the revolutionaries were beyond control, Agrippa II left Jerusalem and withdrew to his own kingdom of Chalcis in the north.

Supported by the lesser priests and encouraged by the revolutionaries, Eleazar, Captain of the Temple, now persuaded those who officiated in the Temple services to reject, and thus halt the making of, the sacrifice which had been offered twice daily for sixty years on behalf of the Emperor and people of Rome. It was, in effect, a repudiation of allegiance tantamount to rebellion.

The rejection of the sacrifice may not have been as straightforward as Josephus reported. According to the *Talmud*, the Jews acted with typical subtlety. Those citizens whose duty it was to produce the sacrificial animal selected a blemished one, anticipating that it would be rejected and so give rise to a charge of disloyalty. The desire of the 'sages', doctors of the

Law, to accept the imperfect animal, clearly with the intention of frustrating the trick, was bitterly contested by a man named Zechariah, who fought successfully to prevent acceptance. If Zechariah was the same man whom Josephus later describes as a Zealot leader, the story suggests that the Zealots may either have forced Eleazar's hand or have collaborated with him into tricking the officiating priests.

Whatever dark motives lay behind the rejection of the sacrifice, the war was officially begun by the act of the fiery son of the former High Priest. His father, Ananias, had persecuted the lesser priests and had turned them into bitter enemies of the pro-Roman regime. Eleazar's desertion of his own class at this moment is usually attributed to the zeal of youth. He may have become infected by the Zealot ideal, although he rejected the leadership of men whom he considered his social inferiors.

As a member of the priestly hierarchy, Eleazar was a notable prize to be won by the disgruntled priests and revolutionaries. Could they have persuaded or tricked Eleazar into igniting the fuse, perhaps by adopting him as their puppet leader? If that was their intention, they were disappointed, for the young man showed energy, resourcefulness, and a keen comprehension of the Zealot threat to his position.

'The principal citizens, the chief priests and the most notable Pharisees' appealed over Eleazar's head to the ultimate and traditional authority. The mass of the people were summoned to assemble in the Temple forecourt, before the bronze gate of the Sanctuary, where, according to both Josephus and Talmudic tradition, the question of the loyal sacrifice was fully debated. The pro-Roman chief priests opposed the disruption of this link with Rome. The Zealots welcomed it. The reaction of the Pharisees is more difficult to discern. In theory they did not approve of foreign rule. They were prepared to put up with it as long as Jewish religious institutions were left undisturbed. They were concerned, not with government, but with personal conduct and the interpretation of the religious Law, to which they now turned for guidance.

On the fundamental question as to whether it was right to accept sacrifices offered by non-Jews, Pharasaic opinion was sharply divided. Some 'priestly experts on the tradition' stated that 'all their ancestors had accepted the sacrifice of aliens'. Others must have voiced a contrary opinion. Josephus claims emphatically in his book *Contra Apion* (his defence of Judaism) that the loyal sacrifice was wholly exceptional in Jewish usage and was improper. The argument raged pro and con. Some speakers took the prudent view that the repudiation of the sacrifice would inevitably lead to war; others declared that it would open the Jews to the charge of deplorable exclusiveness. The learned doctor Jonathan ben Zakkai tactfully suggested that the rejection of the sacrifice should not be considered as a slight on the Romans. He considered that 'moral goodness atones for the Gentiles just as sacrifice atones for the Jews.' He meant that the Romans did not *need* to offer sacrifice, and that rejection did not imply repudiation of the alliance. Jonathan was opposed by the priest Hananiah. He maintained that repudiation of the alliance would lead to anarchy. He appealed to his hearers, 'Pray for the welfare of the Empire; but [meaning except] for the fear thereof men would swallow one another alive.' Hananiah showed a remarkable understanding of his own people.

The most distinguished Pharisee was Simon, the son of that Gamaliel who, twenty years before, had advised the Sanhedrin to leave the Christians alone. He probably did not commit himself at the debate: 'All my days I have grown up among the wise and I have found nought better than silence.' Whosoever is profuse of words causes sin, was his aphorism.

Josephus fails to record the verdict of the assembled people, but the majority obviously welcomed the extremists' action. At the end of the debate, Eleazar and his adherents besieged the Roman garrisons, occupying the Antonia fortress and the royal palace.

The tiny Jewish nation had thrown down the gauntlet to the Roman colossus. To win their freedom, the Jews had shown that they were ready to suffer any torment. God alone was their Lord, and rather than submit to a mortal master, they were prepared to die. The teaching of Judas, the Galilean Messiah, had at last borne fruit. He was long dead but a new leader stood ready to carry on the crusade. Gathering his Zealots, Judas's surviving son Menahem marched from Jerusalem on Masada, the Roman-held fortress on the Dead Sea.

PART II
The Battle of Jerusalem, A.D. 66-70

Nine

The Miracle
at Beth-horon

The reaction of the Sadducees was swift and violent. They were anxious to crush the insurrection before it was too late. They sent messengers north to King Agrippa beseeching him to furnish troops. He despatched two thousand horsemen who gained entry into the Upper City, joining the Jewish peace party and their Roman protectors in the royal palace. The insurgents retained their hold on the Lower City and the Temple, mounting an assault on the Antonia. Josephus, who was hiding in the Temple, describes the action:

> Stones and slings were incessantly in action; from one quarter and from the other there was a continuous hail of missiles; sometimes companies even sallied out and there was a hand-to-hand engagement, the insurgents having the superiority in daring, the king's soldiers in skill. The objective of the royal troops was to capture the Temple and to expel those who were polluting the sanctuary; Eleazar and the rebels strove to gain the Upper City in addition to the ground which they held already. So for seven days there was great slaughter on both sides, neither of the combatants surrendering the portion of the town which he occupied.

On the eighth day of the battle a group of *Sicarii*, seizing the opportunity of the Feast of Wood-Carrying, forced their way into the Temple, where their services were enlisted by the priestly revolutionaries. Together they pressed the attacks more fiercely than before, outmatching the peace party in numbers and audacity and forcing them to evacuate the Upper City.

The victors burst in and set fire to the house of Ananias

the High Priest and to the palaces of Agrippa and Bernice; they next carried their combustibles to the public archives, eager to destroy the money-lenders' bonds and to prevent the recovery of debts, in order to win over a host of grateful debtors and to cause a rising of the poor against the rich, sure of impunity. The keepers of the Record Office having fled, they set light to the building. After consuming the sinews of the city in flames, they advanced against their foes; whereupon the notables and chief priests made their escape, some hiding in the underground passages, while others fled with the royal troops to the Palace [of Herod] situated higher up, and instantly shut the gates; among the latter were Ananias the High Priest, his brother Ezekias and the members of the deputation which had been sent to Agrippa. Satisfied with their victory and incendiary proceedings, the insurgents paused for that day.

Two days later, the insurgents stormed the Antonia, putting the Roman cohort to the sword—a notable feat considering the magnitude of the fortress, whatever the strength of the Roman troops. Eleazar's prestige was greatly enhanced. Only Herod's palace remained to be captured, and this they assaulted under a hail of missiles showered down by the royalist and Roman troops. Many besiegers fell beneath the walls of the four bastions. The combat continued incessantly day and night, the insurgents hoping to exhaust the besieged through failure of supplies, the defenders to wear down the besiegers by fatigue.

At this stage Menahem returned triumphant from Masada, where he had overpowered and massacred the Roman garrison. His men well equipped with captured weapons, he entered Jerusalem 'like a veritable king', which is Josephus's scornful way of dismissing Menahem's Messianic claim. The newcomer assumed leadership of the revolt, forcing Eleazar to take second place—to his chagrin and anger. Several factors contributed to Menahem's predominance, short as was its duration. He had scored a notable victory, his men were well armed, and they comprised a cohesive force bound together by the Zealot ideal. He carried the immense prestige of his ancestry as son of the founder of the sect which had spearheaded resistance to foreign rule. Menahem had probably led the Zealots for twenty years, since the crucifixion of his two brothers by Tiberius Alexander. He took charge of the assault on the royal palace.

Lacking siege engines and exposed as they were to the hail of missiles hurled from the walls, the Zealots and their priestly allies, digging from a distance, undermined one of the towers and, after setting alight its supports, retired. When the props were burned the tower collapsed, revealing to the besiegers a second rampart which the Roman soldiers had hastily constructed. This unexpected sight dismayed the revolutionaries, who had thought victory was already theirs. But either the new wall was less strong than it seemed or the defenders had lost heart. They sent a delegation to Menahem, requesting permission to evacuate the palace under treaty. Menahem granted their request, limiting the capitulation to Agrippa's troops and native Jews. Despairing of cutting their way through the great throng before them, the Romans retired to the three towers named Hippicus, Phasael, and Mariamne. Their desertion of their Roman allies failed to save the chief priests. Ananias and his brother Ezekias were hunted down and killed by the Zealots.

The reduction of the palace stronghold and the murder of Ananias, states Josephus, 'inflated and brutalized' Menahem to such an extent that he 'believed himself without a rival in the conduct of affairs and became an insufferable tyrant'. The partisans of Eleazar soon rose against Menahem for

they remarked to each other that, after revolting from the Romans for love of liberty, they ought not to sacrifice their liberty to a Jewish hangman, and to put up with a master who, even though he were to abstain from violence, was anyhow far below themselves, and that if they must have a leader, anyone would be better than Menahem.

They laid plans to attack him. Josephus failed to add that Menahem, by murdering his father and uncle, had incurred Eleazar's hatred. Nor does the historian explain that in the opinion of the middle-class priests the Zealots were socially

89

inferior peasants. Nonetheless, he called Menahem a 'doctor', or learned man, an unusual tribute to his status.

From his place of asylum in the Temple, Josephus watched Menahem, arrayed in royal robes and attended by his party of armed fanatics, enter the Temple to pay his devotions.

> When Eleazar and his companions rushed upon him, and the rest of the people to gratify their rage took up stones and began pelting the arrogant doctor, imagining that his downfall would crush the whole revolt, Menahem and his followers offered a momentary resistance; then, seeing themselves assailed by the whole multitude, they fled withersoever they could; all who were caught were massacred, and a hunt was made for any in hiding. A few succeeded in escaping by stealth to Masada, among others Eleazar, son of Jairus [Jair] and a relative of Menahem, and subsequently despot of Masada. Menahem himself, who had taken refuge on the place called Opel [Ophel] (on the southeastern hill) and there ignominiously concealed himself, was caught, dragged into the open, and after being subjected to all kinds of torture, put to death. His lieutenants, along with Absalom, his most eminent supporter in his tyranny, met with a similar fate.

The murder of Menahem and the discomfiture of the Zealots pleased Josephus, who ventured from the Temple, feeling it safe to consort with the priestly victors. (His biased story of Menahem's end—see the Appendix—requires discussion, because the circumstances surrounding the Zealot leader's death have been taken to support the theory that it was the Zealots rather than the Essenes who lived at Qumran and wrote the Scrolls found there.)

The Zealot survivors, led by Menahem's kinsman, Eleazar, son of Jair, fled to Masada, where they held out for seven years, taking little part in the subsequent campaign in which other Zealots actively participated.

In killing Menahem, the conspirators, says Josephus, had no intention of ending the war, but only of prosecuting it with greater liberty. Again commanded by Eleazar, the Captain of the Temple, they pressed the siege of the palace towers more vigorously than ever, rejecting the entreaties of the Jewish peace party, which Josephus had now joined. 'We were,' he says, 'in a great state of alarm for we saw the people in arms and we were at a loss what to do, being powerless to check the revolutionaries.' Realizing their peril, these citizens professed to concur with the views of the revolutionaries, urging only that they should leave the Romans alone if they sent an army to retake the city; 'in order to gain credit for resorting to arms only in self-defence'. Josephus is, of course, anxious to convince his Roman readers that the part he played in the revolt was conciliatory.

The hostilities within the city were brought to an end by the Romans' offer to capitulate in return for their lives. Upon Eleazar's acceptance of their terms, they marched out of the palace, led by their Commander, Metillius. Josephus, the eye-witness, tells the cruel story:

> So long as the soldiers retained their arms, none of the rebels molested them or gave any indication of treachery; but when, in accordance with the covenant, they had all laid down their bucklers and swords, and, with no suspicion remaining, were taking their departure, Eleazar's party fell upon them, surrounded and massacred them; the Romans neither resisting nor sueing for mercy, but merely appealing with loud cries to 'the covenant' and 'the oaths'. Thus, brutally butchered, perished all save Metillius; he alone saved his life by entreaties and promises to turn Jew, and even to be circumcised.

The injury to the Romans, who had lost a handful of men, was slight. To the peaceful Jewish citizens who had had no part in the slaughter it seemed the prelude to ruin.

> Seeing the grounds for war to be now beyond remedy, and the city polluted by such stain of guilt as could not but arouse a dread of some visitation from heaven, if not of the vengeance of Rome, they gave themselves up to

public mourning; the whole city was a scene of dejection, and among the moderates there was not one who was not wracked with the thought that he would personally have to suffer for the rebels' crime. For, to add to its heinousness, the massacre took place on the Sabbath, a day on which from religious scruples Jews abstain even from the most innocent acts.

Retribution, when it came, was swift and fearful. Throughout Syria and in many parts of Palestine Gentiles massacred Jews, and Jews retaliated by massacring Gentiles, depending upon which held the upper hand in each town and village. Riots broke out in Alexandria where the governor, the former Procurator Tiberius Alexander, 'let loose' two legions and a host of auxiliaries upon the Jews, many of whom were killed.

Aroused at last, for he had delayed taking action for three months, the Legate of Syria, Cestius Gallus, marched from Antioch with a large force consisting of the Twelfth Legion, contingents from other legions, and squadrons of cavalry. A host of auxiliaries were supplied by the three provincial kings, Antiochus of Commagene, Soaemus of Emessa, and Agrippa II. If we are to believe Josephus, Gallus's army numbered about 18,000 men.

Destroying towns and villages and ravaging the countryside, Gallus marched through Galilee and Judaea, reaching the town of Gaba, about eight miles from Jerusalem, in early October. The Jews were gathering in the Holy City to celebrate the Feast of Tabernacles. Learning of Gallus's approach, they abandoned the Feast, rushed to arms, and poured out of the city.

Josephus describes from hearsay the ensuing engagement, in which only part of the Roman army seems to have been involved. It is improbable, unless the Romans had posted considerable numbers of troops to guard communications, that the Jews could have broken and penetrated the Roman ranks, putting their whole army in jeopardy. It was saved only by the spirited action of the cavalry. Suffering only twenty-two casualties, the main body of the Jews fell back to the city. Simon

Gioras, a new leader, harassed the Roman rear guard, cutting off many baggage animals, which he brought in triumph to Jerusalem.

Gallus, who remained in camp for three days, sent envoys to parley with the revolutionaries in an effort to detach non-sympathizers. The Jews killed one envoy before he could utter a word and wounded the other, clubbing and stoning any Jews who protested. Having failed to sow dissension among the enemy, Gallus brought up his army and encamped on Mount Scopus, the hill which overlooks Jerusalem. From there he deployed his army and marched on the city, burning the northern suburb of Bezetha. The Jews retired behind their second wall, and Gallus encamped outside Herod's palace, the three towers of which were held by the Jews, along with the Antonia fortress and the Temple. 'Had he [Gallus],' says Josephus,

> at that particular moment, decided to force his way through the walls, he would have captured the city forthwith, and the war would have been over; but his camp-prefect, Tyrannius Priscus, with most of the cavalry commanders, bribed by [the Procurator] Florus, diverted him from the attempt. Hence it came about that the war was so long protracted and the Jews drained the cup of irretrievable disaster.

Josephus's explanation of Gallus's fatal delay is incomprehensible. Even had Priscus, commander of the Twelfth Legion, been bribed, it is unlikely that he could have swayed his general's decision. Gallus may still have hoped to win the city with the aid of the peace envoys. Yet, according to Josephus, he disbelieved the sincerity of their offer to open the gates. While he hesitated, the revolutionaries pulled his allies from the walls and drove them into their houses, posting themselves on the palace bastions.

Josephus's story of Gallus's attempt to recapture Jerusalem is incoherent—as he may have intended it to be for some obscure personal reason. He fails to explain, for example, how members of the Jewish peace party gained access to an unguarded tower or why Gallus mistrusted the offer to open the gates, preferring rather the Herculean task of scaling the city walls.

Unable to secure the palace, one of the city's three strong-points, Gallus switched his assault to the 'north side of the Temple', an ambiguous description which may refer to either the outer wall which surrounded the Temple precincts or to the Sanctuary itself. The Jews resisted the attack from the 'roof of the portico', which could have described either the portico beneath the outer wall, or one of those surrounding the Sanctuary. Josephus also failed to state whether the Romans had assaulted the Antonia fortress at the north-western corner of the Temple platform, a reference which might have provided a guide through the maze of his narrative.

For five days the Romans attempted to scale the wall, being repulsed time after time. At length the defenders, overpowered by the hail of missiles, gave way. Forming a *testudo*—the device of locking their shields over their heads to protect themselves—the Roman soldiers undermined the wall and attempted to set fire to the gate. A terrible panic seized the defenders, many of whom sought to escape from the city, believing it to be on the verge of capture. Whereupon 'the people', as Josephus calls the peace-seekers, sought to open the gates and welcome Gallus as a benefactor.

But, failing to recognize the despair of the defenders, Gallus suddenly suspended the assault and without suffering any reverse abandoned the siege—'contrary to all expectation'.

No historian has succeeded in supplying any adequate reason for Gallus's strange and disastrous decision. He did not lack siege engines, since the Jews are recorded as capturing them during his retreat. He had secured his supply line during his advance on Jerusalem. In that arid region he may have run out of water. He may have lost his nerve—a likely possibility, to judge by his subsequent fate. He may have feared that, having captured the city, he might himself become besieged. He may have been persuaded by Florus's bribe.

Gallus withdrew his army to Mount Scopus, whither he was followed by the Jews. Plucking up their courage, the insurgents fell upon his rear, killing a number of cavalry and infantry. Next day Gallus continued his retreat, still harassed by the Jews, who hung upon his heels, pouring missiles on the flanks of his column. Whether or not Josephus joined the pursuers, he supplied his readers with a vivid description of the action:

> The rear ranks did not dare to round upon those who were wounding them from behind, supposing that they were pursued by an innumerable host; nor did the rest venture to beat off those who were pressing their flanks, being heavily armed themselves and afraid of opening out their ranks, while the Jews, as they saw, were light-armed and prepared to dash in among them. The result was that they suffered heavily, without any retaliation upon their foes. All along the route men were continually being struck, torn from the ranks, and dropping on the ground. At length, after numerous casualties, including Priscus, the commander of the Sixth Legion, Longinus, a tribune, and Acmilius Jucundus, a commander of a troop of horse, with difficulty the army reached their former camp at Gabao [Gaba], having further abandoned the greater part of their baggage. Here Cestius halted for two days, uncertain what course to pursue; but, on the third, seeing the enemy's strength greatly increased and all the surrounding country swarming with Jews, he decided that the delay had been detrimental to him, and, if further prolonged, would but increase the number of his foes.

Cestius Gallus turned from the road that led directly northwards from Jerusalem in order to follow the more westerly route to Caesarea. By taking that branch he would soon leave the hills behind and reach the maritime plain, where his disciplined soldiers, and particularly his cavalry, could fight to better advantage. At Gaba he was still on the range of hills which run north and south, and on which Jerusalem is situated. The road (where I have retraced the course of the battle) runs along the summit of these hills, following their contours, dipping, rising, and curving. On both sides of the road the country is bare and open. Nowhere, by any stretch of the imagination, is there now a place that can be called a 'defile', the term employed by Josephus to describe the site of the battle. Between the villages of Beth-horon Superior and Beth-horon Inferior (the Arab villages of Beit Ur el Tahta and Beit Ur el Fauqua), where the Twelfth Legion was virtually and unaccountably annihilated, there is no trace of such a trap. Between these villages, the road dips five hundred feet into a wide and open cross-valley, from where it ascends gradually before turning sharply to the right past the farther village. It was past these two Beth-horons that Joshua pursued the Canaanite kings (*Joshua* 10:10) and Beth-horon was the scene of Judas Maccabaeus's triumph over the Seleucid army, two famous victories which may have inspired the Jews.

Possibly the terrain looked very different nineteen hundred years ago. A photograph published as recently as 1937 (C. Ricciolti, *La Guerra Guidaica*, Vol. II, page 351) depicts a scene which recent road construction may have changed. Whether or not Josephus exaggerated the contours in A.D. 66, the ridges and declivities must have provided excellent cover for an attacking force skilled in guerilla tactics.

The disaster that befell the Roman punitive expedition there on November 23 was the greatest calamity the Roman army had suffered since A.D. 9, when Varus lost his legions and his life in the Teutobergwald in north-western Germany.

> To accelerate the retreat he [Gallus] gave orders to retrench all impediments. So the mules, asses, and all the beasts of burden were killed, excepting those that carried missiles and engines of war; these they clung to for their own use, and, still more, from fear of their falling into Jewish hands, and being employed against themselves. Cestius then led his army on down the road to Beth-horon. On the open ground their movements were less harassed by the Jews, but, once the Romans became involved in the defiles and had begun the descent, one party of the enemy went ahead of them and barred their egress, another drove the rear guard down into the ravine, while the main body lined the heights above the narrowest part of the route and covered the legions with showers of arrows. Here, while

even the infantry were hard put to defend themselves, the cavalry were in still greater jeopardy; to advance in order down the road under the hail of darts was impossible, to charge up the slopes was impracticable for horses; on either side were precipices and ravines, down which they slipped and were hurled to destruction; there was no room for flight, no conceivable means of defence; in their utter helplessness the troops were reduced to groans and the wailings of despair, which were answered by the war-whoop of the Jews, with mingled shouts of exultation and fury. Cestius and his entire army were, indeed, within an ace of being captured; only the intervention of night enabled the Romans to find refuge in Beth-horon. The Jews occupied all the surrounding points and kept a look-out for their departure.

The Romans and their allies had encamped for the night at Beth-horon Inferior, where they lay surrounded by the Jews, who occupied the slopes but who failed to advance ahead of the enemy in order to cut the Roman retreat to Lydda (the modern Lod) and to Caesarea.

Despairing of his march, Gallus laid plans for secret flight. Selecting four hundred of his bravest men, he posted them on the roofs of the houses, ordering them to call their watches as usual to deceive the Jews while the army crept stealthily away. Discovering at daybreak that the Romans had fled, the Jews annihilated the gallant four hundred and hastened in pursuit of Gallus. Having stolen a march on his enemies, the Legate quickened his flight, keeping up such a pace that his soldiers were forced to abandon their battering rams, catapults, and other machines. These were seized by the Jews, who turned them upon their foes. But they failed to halt the Romans, so, carrying their spoils and singing songs of triumph, they returned to Jerusalem. They had slain, states Josephus, 5,300 infantry and 480 cavalry, and their own losses had been small. The new Zealot leader, yet another Eleazar, the son of Simon, captured the Roman pay chest, which he carried off in triumph.

From Josephus's description of the battle, we can only assume that, caught in undulating ground too rough for cavalry, the heavily encumbered slow-moving legionaries fell victim to the guerilla tactics of the elusive Jews, who harassed the column, dispersing when the Romans counterattacked and re-forming when they resumed their march.

Following his retreat, states Tacitus, Gallus died, though whether 'in the course of nature or from vexation' the historian did not know.

The Jewish revolutionaries had won a great victory. Once again God had come to their aid, as He had saved Jerusalem in 701 B.C. from Sennacherib's army. Josephus wrote in later life that the reverse suffered by Gallus proved in the long run disastrous for the Jews, since 'those who were bent on war were thereby still more elated, and having once defeated the Romans, hoped to continue victorious to the end'.

Ten

The Roman
and Jewish Generals

The Emperor Nero was visiting Greece when he heard the news of the Roman defeat. It filled him with consternation and alarm —which he hid from the general public (towards whom he affected an attitude of contempt and indignation). The unfortunate incident was due, Nero announced, to failure of generalship rather than to Jewish valour. Nevertheless, the revolt was a serious matter, for it could lead to a flare-up throughout the East among the widespread Jewish Diaspora. Roman prestige was at stake. The reconquest of Judaea would be a long and costly job, and the Roman army was already fully extended.

To guard their Empire, which then extended from the Euphrates to Britain, the Romans had adopted the policy of linear rather than mobile defence—and for good reason, since contemporary methods of transport were too slow for easy manoeuvre. The Roman armies were therefore strung out along their 4,000 miles of land frontiers. To protect the East, three legions were stationed in Syria and two in Egypt. In A.D. 66 Nero was planning two great expeditions, one to crush the Albani on the shores of the Caspian Sea, and another to penetrate Ethiopia. The revolt of the chieftain Vindex in Gaul caused the abandonment of the first, and the outbreak of the Jewish rebellion led to the cancellation of the second.

Even when its legions stood at full strength, the Roman army was small in relation to its manifold duties. Its 168,000 soldiers were mobilized in 28 legions, with two more, perhaps, in a state of semi-mobilization or disintegration. The Twelfth Legion, called the *Fulminata* from the place of its origin, had been badly cut up at Beth-horon and had lost its Eagle. Its morale was low. Auxiliaries were recruited locally, chiefly horsemen and archers.

Each legion constituted a complete miniature army, supplied with cavalry and bowmen and trained and equipped to campaign on its own. Its paper strength was about 6,000 men, officered by Centurions and Tribunes, and commanded by a *Legatus*, a man of senatorial rank. A soldier served for twenty-five years. Upon discharge he was granted a plot of land either in his own country or in the locality in which his legion served. Few, if any, of the legions were entirely Roman in composition, but whatever their racial origin, the soldiers were bound by strict discipline. For even the slightest neglect of duty the punishment was death. It was this discipline that gave the Roman army its strength and character. Some legions were better trained and disciplined than others; those raised in the East were reckoned inferior to those recruited in Europe.

The Romans had no powerful enemies; their opponents were either small, ill-organized nations or barbarian tribes. No strong state now existed to challenge Rome, or threaten its Empire. On their frontiers, the Romans might lose the first battle but were bound to win the war. Suppression of revolt required only time and money, and Nero, with all his extravagances, was short of cash. This difficulty was overcome somehow, and the army of the East was put on a war footing very quickly, due to the superb organizing ability of the Roman bureaucracy. The clerks in Rome dealt with pay and allowances, and operated a soldiers' savings bank, into which they could deposit sums saved from their annual pay of 120 *denarii*, half of which was held for food and clothing, and from their share of booty. Officers were highly paid, a Centurion receiving 5,000 *denarii*, a Tribune 20,000, and a Legate 30,000. Inevitably, these funds whetted the greed of indigent Emperors. Domitian stole the funds for his own purposes.

Each soldier was uniformly armed, wearing an iron-link cuirass and backplate, iron helmet, and heavy hob-nailed boots. He carried a shield, a sword, a dagger, and a javelin—the *pilum*, which during the first century had evolved from a defensive weapon into an easily thrown lance. Then as now, weapons dictated tactics, and the legion fought in a compact mass, mobility and firepower being provided by the hosts of auxiliaries.

The horsemen still lacked the stirrup which, when it was introduced into Europe in the seventh century, gave cohesion to cavalry manoeuvres. The archers were armed with the 'composite' bow, formed of two bows lashed end to end to provide greater torsion. The old 'simple' bow may have been used by less civilized peoples. The range of the composite bow was less than it has been given credit for. The light 'practice' arrow could be fired for 250 yards, the heavy 'war' arrow was effective only up to 150 or 200 yards.

Each legion carried, and may have individually constructed, its own artillery, which consisted of two types of machine: the *catapulta* derived its power from springs and could fling stones, arrows and spears with great impact; the torsion-operated *ballista* hurled bolts and stone shot. These weapons were very accurate, as Josephus points out in his account of the Siege of Jerusalem. Their capabilities will be described in greater detail in the account of the great battle, as well as those of the Roman *testudo*, and their battering-rams. The artillery was constructed, serviced, and operated by a special corps of artificers, men who were accorded unique status and rank. Such weaponry was limited only by lack of the skilled workmen required. On the march these arms were loaded on carriages, or transported unassembled on animals. In addition, each legion carried entrenching tools, bridging equipment with which to span streams and small rivers, and the implements for constructing fortified camps—a legion's first task on arriving at its destination.

To command the army for the re-conquest of Palestine, Nero selected fifty-seven-year-old veteran general Vespasian. He had won great renown in Britain, where with his son Titus he had campaigned under Aulus Plautius, fighting thirty battles, subjugating thirty belligerent tribes, and capturing more than twenty towns, as well as subduing the Isle of Wight. Previously he had served in Thrace, Crete, and Cyrenaica and on his elevation to the rank of Consul had received the governorship of North Africa. There, states Seutonius, 'his rule was characterized by justice and great dignity'; and from there he returned home 'no richer than he went'. It was his misfortune to have offended Nero deeply by falling asleep during one of the Emperor's theatrical performances, and consequently, in some fear for his life, he had lately lived in country retirement—from which he was recalled to take command in Judaea. A large, slow-thinking man, Vespasian was now re-appraised by his sovereign as the best man for the job, an active and competent soldier who could be trusted with great, and possibly dangerous, power.

Having crossed the Hellespont, Vespasian travelled overland to Syria, where he took command of two legions, the Fifth and Tenth, as well as the remnant of the Twelfth, and where later he was joined by Titus. According to Josephus, Vespasian assembled a host of auxiliaries comprising twenty-three cohorts and squadrons of cavalry. Ten of these numbered a thousand men, and thirteen had a strength of 600 infantry and 120 cavalry. The provincial kings Antiochus, Agrippa, and Soaemus each provided 2,000 unmounted bowmen and 1,000 cavalry; the Arab King Malchus sent 1,000 cavalry and 5,000 infantry, chiefly bowmen. The total strength of the force, Josephus estimated, was 60,000 soldiers without counting servants. Whatever the exact figure may have been, it was a formidable array.

The Jews were hardly prepared to counter this army of disciplined regulars and royal troops. They possessed no regular army, no arsenal, and their men were ill-trained, ill-disciplined, and divided by faction. They were experienced only in guerilla warfare, but, buoyed by hope and fanatical zeal, they determined to take the initiative. During the winter they made preparations to defend their freedom.

Following the victory of the rebels at Beth-horon, many eminent men had to flee Jerusalem. Simon Gioras, who had fought so well against Gallus, was driven from Jerusalem by the priestly junta and fled with his band of revolutionaries to Masada. There he temporarily joined the Zealots commanded by Eleazar, the son of Jair, though Simon Gioras himself was not a Zealot. He had gathered a large personal following in northern Judaea, and he had a distinct policy of his own. He was not at first welcomed by Eleazar, though later the two leaders collaborated in raids on the countryside to gather supplies. The other Zealot leader, Eleazar the son of Simon, despite

the prominent part he had played at Beth-horon, was also excluded from power in Jerusalem.

The loyalties and party affiliations of the Jews during the
revolt are difficult to determine. Josephus fails to explain Jewish
ideological differences, which he may have though incomprehensible to his Roman readers. He merely attributes to each
popular leader the unworthy motive of personal ambition; but
each chieftain probably founded his own party on some principle,
however determined each may have been to become dominant.
Starting as a middle-class revolt, the Jewish insurrection developed into a class struggle. Leaders were able to control the rest-
less mass of people, who were as anxious to free themselves from
the sacerdotal nobility as they were to win their freedom from
Roman rule.

The term 'revolutionaries', which Josephus freely uses, had
wide meaning. Several partisan bands probably shared the
Zealots' religious and political motivations. There were also
other visionary groups, such as the Essenes and Messianists,
whose participation in the revolt is less certain.

The Zealots claimed to be the élite of these revolutionary
groups. They were probably far fewer than is supposed. They
had split into two factions: the Jerusalemite Zealots, followers
of Eleazar the son of Simon, who stayed in the city and fought
in its defence; and those who had fled to Masada with Menahem's kinsman, Eleazar the son of Jair. The Masada Zealots
considered themselves the true inheritors of Zealotism. Their
exclusiveness apparently barred them from assisting their com-
patriots in their death struggle with Rome.

On the death of Menahem, control of the revolution in Jerusalem had reverted to the aristocratic Eleazar, the Temple
Captain. Now, suddenly and unexpectedly, the power was seized
by a priestly junta who instituted a provisional government and
got rid of the fiery Captain Eleazar by fobbing him off with an
unimportant command.

Why Eleazar allowed himself to be superseded and cast aside
by the pro-Roman priestly aristocrats, the very men against
whose rule he had instigated his revolt, is beyond understanding. We can only suppose that the chief priests, re-asserting

their traditional hegemony, intended to guide the revolt into channels which might keep negotiations open with the Romans.

Whatever dark intrigues may have lain behind Eleazar's removal from power, the forces of law and order then took over a situation which had probably threatened anarchy. Only the High Priests, as the nation's representatives with God, could invoke the traditional authority of the Sanhedrin. The current incumbent, Mattathias, nominee of the renegade Agrippa, was, however, a nonentity. Into the vacuum stepped Ananus, the 'rash and daring' Sadducee who had been High Priest briefly during the procuratorial interregnum in A.D. 62. With Ananus was appointed a layman named Joseph, son of Gorian, whom Ananus manoeuvred into a position of obscurity. Strangely, they were joined by the taciturn Pharisee, Simon the son of Gamaliel, who opposed the war. Ananus may have included Simon in his government to give his policy the semblance of Pharasaic approval and to channel the revolt to his own advantage. Of the other living ex-High Priests, Ishmael ben Phabi was held hostage in Rome, and Jesus ben Gamala, Joseph ben Simon Kabi, and Jesus ben Dimmia remained in Jerusalem.

Ananus retained the former machinery of administration, minting coinage which bore the inscription JERUSALEM THE HOLY and was stamped, according to the date, the FIRST, SECOND, etc., YEAR OF REDEMPTION. He appointed officials, controlled the use of public funds, and enforced the payment of taxes. He was careful to adopt the constitutional forms of theocratic government. The High Priest stood at the apex, listening to the advice of the Sanhedrin, that State Council and highest court formed of Sadducees and prominent Pharisees. The guerilla leaders were excluded.

Traditionally, ultimate authority rested in the people, through the 'popular assembly' summoned to the Temple's forecourt as it had been following the rejection of the loyal sacrifice. Now it convened to hear Ananus's proposals and to confirm the council's appointment of generals to wage the war.

The assembled people, states the eyewitness historian, elected as joint generals Ananus and Joseph son of Gorian. Seven lesser generals were appointed to command districts. Jesus, the son of

Sapias, and Eleazar Captain of the Temple—the man who had
instigated the revolt—were sent to Idumaea, to the south of
Judaea. There they were joined by Niger, a native of Peraea.
Joseph son of Simon commanded at Jericho, Manasseh at Peraea,
and John the Essene at Thamna, with Lydda, Emmaus (in the
Martime Plain), and Joppa also under his charge. John son of
Ananias was given Gophna and Achrabatta (northern Judaea),
and the youthful Josephus was sent to Galilee and to the city
of Gamala, east of the Sea of Galilee. His appointment
may have stemmed from his experience in Rome where, he
claims, he had studied Roman military organization, knowledge
which may have been welcomed.

While these generals journeyed to take up their commands,
Ananus occupied himself in Jerusalem, heightening the city's
walls, completing the Third Wall which King Agrippa had left
unfinished, accumulating engines of war, and setting craftsmen
to construct weapons and missiles. He welded a mass of young
men into an army by what Josephus contemptuously calls
'desultory training'. The whole was 'one scene of tumult':

> On the other side, the dejection of the moderates was pro-
> found; and many, foreseeing the impending disasters, made
> open lamentations. Then, too, there were omens, which to
> the friends of peace boded ill, although those who had
> kindled the war readily invented favourable interpretations
> for them. In short, the city before the coming of the Romans
> wore the appearance of a place doomed to destruction.
> Ananus, nevertheless, cherished the thought of gradually
> abandoning these warlike preparations and bending the
> malcontents and the infatuated so-called Zealots to a more
> salutary policy; but he succumbed to their violence.

Generals Niger and John the Essene (whose supposedly pacific
principles did not keep him from joining the revolt) marched
upon Ascalon, sixty miles by road to the south-west of Jerusalem. The ancient maritime town was guarded by a Roman
cohort and a squadron of cavalry. Antonius, the Roman commander, easily dispersed the Jewish army, killing John. Re-

assembling his forces, Niger renewed the attack. Antonius laid ambuscades in the mountain passes into which the inexperienced Jews marched. They took refuge in a fortified tower. The Romans set it on fire. The Jews retreated, believing that Niger had perished in the flames. Not so, however, for he had found refuge in a cave in the recesses of the fortress, where later his lamenting friends, searching for his body for burial, found him. And, says Josephus, 'his reappearance filled all Jewish hearts with unlooked-for joy, for they thought that God's providence had preserved him to be their General in the conflict to come'.

Eleven

Civil War

Josephus took up his command in Galilee as the accredited representative of the Jerusalem government. He and the local partisan leader, John of Gischala, became implacable enemies. Each man accused the other of disloyalty to the government. Josephus called John an opportunist who had seized upon the revolt to further his own ambitions. He describes him as 'the most unscrupulous and crafty of all who have gained notoriety by such unsavoury means'. John spread the report that Josephus 'intended to betray the country to the Romans' and sent secret envoys to denounce him in Jerusalem.

Subsequent events proved John right. He tried to persuade Ananus to 'clip' Josephus's 'sprouting wings'. Influenced by the Pharisee Simon, a friend of John's, Ananus sent an armed force to Galilee to expel Josephus. But Josephus outmanoeuvred his antagonists, who were forced to return crestfallen to Jerusalem.

The historian's ambiguous story of his role in Galilee reveals one important fact. John of Gischala, whom he called a 'bandit', was in reality a notable Pharisee, for he would not otherwise have gained Simon's friendship.

Behind these plots and counterplots lay deep intrigues, at the nature of which we can only guess. Did Josephus and Ananus connive to end the revolt? Was their plot detected and disclosed by John and Simon? Another incident which occurred about this time indicates Ananus's state of mind: he despatched an expedition to northern Judaea to oust Simon Gioras, who had returned to his home province of Acrabathane. Clearly, Ananus intended to keep control of the revolt.

The private feud in Galilee between Josephus and John was brought to an end by the advance of the Romans, who reached Ptolemaïs on the sea coast in June, A.D. 67. John, after defending his native town of Gischala, fled to Jerusalem. Josephus took charge in the town of Jotapata, a very strong fortress perched on the top of a hill. According to his own history, he courageously defended the fort for forty-seven days against Vespasian's assault. (In this instance he could hardly have lied, since after the publication of his history Vespasian, by then the Roman Emperor, vouched for its truth.)

When the Romans broke into the town, massacring its defenders, Josephus took refuge in a cave, joining forty other survivors whom he tried to persuade to surrender, whereupon they threatened to kill him and then themselves. Pretending to fall in with their plan, he proposed drawing lots to decide who should be the last to die. As each man drew a blank, he presented his throat to be cut until, at last, only two men remained alive, Josephus and another. Unable, he says, to stain his hands with Jewish blood, Josephus persuaded the other survivor to surrender.

Brought before Vespasian, with whom he was granted a private interview, Josephus predicted that Vespasian and his son Titus after him would become Emperors of Rome. He referred to the Jewish oracle, well known to the Romans, which foretold that a man from Judaea was destined to become the ruler of the world. Sceptical as he may have been, Vespasian was sufficiently superstitious to place some reliance upon Josephus, whom he knew to have made other predictions which had come true. He spared the visionary's life and ordered him to be held captive, though treating him with kindness.

The news of the fall of Jotapata and of Josephus's defection was received in Jerusalem with incredulity—and mounting indignation when it became known that he almost alone of its defenders had survived. He was cursed as a coward and a traitor, a charge which became magnified into the allegation of a priestly plot to sell out to the Romans. The part played by John of Gischala in these intrigues is uncertain. Josephus says that John was elected to command the war party in Jerusalem. Later he collaborated with the priests who valued his influence with the people, and whose secret counsels he betrayed to the Zealots.

If Josephus is to be believed, the situation in Jerusalem was chaotic. He writes about it from hearsay, his narrative is filled with inconsistencies, and his sympathies lie with his aristocratic friends who opposed the extreme nationalists, according to him, villains of the blackest dye. He lumps together all the 'so-called Zealots', as he contemptuously calls the patriots, some of whom may have been the true patriots and others the desperados, he alleges.

Josephus's treachery had compromised the priestly junta, who were now assailed by the 'enthusiasts for war', as the historian called the Zealots and other partisans. Each faction strove to achieve its own military dictatorship within Jerusalem. The anti-government party increased in strength as they were joined by other partisan leaders driven into the city by the Roman advance.

Emboldened by their great strength, the Zealots and their allies murdered the 'most eminent men', causing 'such dire panic as if the city had been captured by the enemy'. It seemed a better fate, remarks Josephus, to be taken prisoner by the Romans than to fall victim to one's friends. The old and prudent mourned for the city, as if it had already met its doom. John stirred up the malcontents, the reckless youths, inciting them to war and ridiculing the power of the Romans. For their monstrous crimes, says Josephus, the Zealots invented the equally monstrous excuse that their victims had plotted the surrender of Jerusalem and had to be slain as the enemies of liberty. They boasted of their murders as if they were the benefactors of the people.

In the eyes of their priestly opponents, the Zealots committed an even more terrible crime when they reverted to ancient practice and elected their own High Priest. They selected by lot an illiterate peasant named Phinehas, decking him in the sacred vestments. Josephus says he was totally ignorant and incapable of exercising this office, but Phinehas in his new guise was recognized by the leading Pharisees. According to Talmudic references, Phinehas was related to Simon son of Gamaliel by marriage. Stirred into action by this mockery, Ananus led his citizen army in an attack on the Zealots, forcing them to retreat within the Temple. By their apathy they had created a monster, he told the people, and urged them to resist the internal threat to their liberty as bravely as they had defied the lords of the inhabited world. They must destroy the Zealots *now* rather than wait for the Romans to deliver God's Sanctuary.

Informed by spies of the threat to their fortress, the Zealots under Eleazar son of Simon sallied out, striking down all who stood in their path. Caught unawares, the citizens at first were no match for their reckless opponents. But, as their numbers grew and were roused to fury, they threw their whole force upon their enemies. Unable to stand the pressure, the Zealots withdrew into the Temple, barring the gates behind them.

John of Gischala betrayed the citizens' plans to the Zealots, whose knowledge of his intentions raised Ananus's suspicions. Believing John too powerful to destroy, Ananus forced him to take an oath of allegiance to the popular cause. Now satisfied of his loyalty, he sent John to negotiate with the Zealots. Admitted to the Temple, John broke his oath and for treacherous reasons falsely informed Eleazar that Ananus had sent an embassy to Vespasian, inviting him to enter the city. To gain possession of the Temple, said John, Ananus intended to infiltrate his soldiers among the worshippers at the coming Feast. 'You cannot hold the Temple without allies.' John warned the Zealots, and he advised them to call upon the Idumaeans, the tribe who lived in the south of Judaea. Taking his advice, Eleazar sent two envoys, both fleet of foot and persuasive talkers, to enlist the aid of the Idumaean leader, Simon. The Idumaeans, the Arab tribe from whom Herod the Great had sprung, were, says Josephus, 'turbulent and disorderly people' who delighted in revolutionary changes. Easily persuaded to join their co-religionists' revolt, they marched on Jerusalem.

Learning of their approach, Ananus shut the city gates, forcing the Idumaeans to camp outside the walls. That night a terrible thunderstorm broke over Jerusalem. The thunder pealed and the rain poured down in sheets, soaking the Idumaeans to the skin as they huddled together for warmth. Within the Temple Eleazar and John, who had not returned to Ananus, conferred, seeking a way to admit their allies. The shattering rain had forced the citizen sentries to take shelter. Creeping through the deserted streets, a small band of Zealots, their footsteps cloaked by the thunder and blustering wind, reached and unbarred a gate. They led the Idumaeans to the Temple. Next day Ananus recognized their swarthy faces as they guarded the walls above. His cries of alarm were deadened by the persistent storm. Too late he rushed to arouse the citizens to their danger.

The Zealots and Idumaeans erupted from the Temple, catching their enemies unawares and massacring all who resisted. Many people cast away their arms and took refuge in their houses, whither the Zealots followed, killing and looting. They searched particularly for the chief priests, finding and slaying Ananus and his main supporter—next in the priestly hierarchy —and casting out their bodies without burial, a terrible impiety.

The Roman capture of the city began with the death of Ananus; Josephus dated the downfall of the Jewish state from that day. Having disposed of the leaders, the Zealots and Idumaean hordes butchered the people 'as though they had been a herd of unclean animals'. Ordinary folk were slain on the spot; the young nobles were offered their lives if they would join the Zealot cause. They refused, and they too were tortured and killed. To such conditions were the people reduced that none dared to weep or bury their dead. Even within doors they stifled their tears so their lamentations would not be detected by their enemies.

Anxious to justify their allegation that the priests had plotted to open the city gates to the Romans, the Zealots staged a mock trial in the Temple. A rich man named Zacharias was charged with treasonable correspondence with the enemy. To give the trial the semblance of legality, seventy leading citizens were summoned to act as judges. These the Zealots sought to persuade by eloquence rather than by evidence. Springing to his feet, Zacharias turned on his accusers, ridiculing the proceedings and describing the enormities committed by the Zealots. They tried to drown his voice by uproar. Refusing to be intimidated, the heroic seventy acquitted Zacharias, whereupon two Zealots killed him with their swords.

This atrocity sickened their Idumaean allies, who, states Josephus, took offence. Their mood was heightened by the revelations of a certain Zealot who described other crimes his party had committed. Believing that they had been duped—for no evidence had emerged that the priests had plotted to surrender the city—most of the Idumaeans departed from Jerusalem in disgust, leaving the Zealots in command. They celebrated their victory by more murders, killing one Gorion—possibly the Gorion who had joined Simon ben Gamaliel in his intrigues against the Zealots—and Niger the Peraean, hero of the attack on Ascalon.

> This veteran was dragged through the midst of the city. When brought without the gates, he, despairing of his life, besought them to give him burial; but they fiercely declared that they would not grant him the one desire of his heart— a grave—and then proceeded to murder him. In his dying moments Niger called upon their heads the vengeance of the Romans, famine and pestilence to add to the horrors of war, and, to crown all, internecine strife.

Niger's removal and other murders were called 'liquidation of traitors' by the Zealots. They were left without formidable rivals, and they reigned supreme in Jerusalem. But who would rule the Zealots?

Aerial photograph of Jerusalem taken from the South shows the Temple platform on the right, with the Moslem Mosque in the centre. To the left of the Temple ran the outer valley and to its left again rose the Upper City which was dominated by the three towers of Herod's Palace. North of the city the ground rises to Mount Scopus. The Hinnom and Kidron valleys encircle the West, South and East. The Mount of Olives rises to the East of the Kidron.

Israel Press Office

above South-eastern corner of the Temple Walls—the 'Pinnacle'. *By courtesy of the Israel Department of Antiquities and Museums*

below The remaining and partly Herodian Tower of the Citadel which was once Herod's Palace. *By courtesy of the Israel Department of Antiquities and Museums*

above The South Wall of the Temple which shows the 1968 excavations to ground level. *Israel Exploration Society*

below Detail from the Arch of Titus in the Roman Forum depicting the spoils of Jerusalem carried in the Triumph of A.D. 71. *Israel Press Office*

above View of Masada shown from the West. This rock fortress was defended by the Zealots in A.D. 73. The Roman ramp reached to the top until 1927 when an earthquake caused a small slide. The outlines of two of the Roman camps can be seen. *Israel Press Office*

right The *Ivdaea Capta*—a coin struck by the Romans as a potent instrument of propaganda to demonstrate throughout their far-flung Empire the folly of revolt. *The Israel Museum*

Twelve

Hiding the
Temple Treasure

Vespasian learned of the dissensions in Jerusalem. Despite the entreaties of his officers to assault the city 'before the Jews returned to unanimity', he refused to be deterred from his purpose —the slow and inexorable subjection of the country. An immediate advance, he told his staff, would merely unite their opponents. They would do best to wait until the Jews had wasted their strength by civil war.

The soundness of Vespasian's judgment was soon made evident by the number of Jews who daily deserted the city. Not all succeeded in reaching the Roman camp, so great was the Zealots' vigilance. Anyone caught outside the city wall was arrested on the assumption that he was going off to join the Romans. The rich were allowed to buy their freedom. The poor were slaughtered. The highways became piled with dead. The penalty for burying the body of a relative executed as a traitor or deserter, Josephus says, was death:

> Such terror prevailed that the survivors deemed blessed the lot of the earlier victims, now at rest, while the tortured wretches in the prisons pronounced even the unburied happy in comparison with themselves. Every human ordinance was trampled under foot, every dictate of religion ridiculed by these men, who scoffed at the oracles of the prophets as impostors' fables. Yet those predictions of theirs contained much concerning virtue and vice, by the transgression of which the Zealots brought upon their country the fulfilment of the prophecies directed against it. For there was an ancient saying of inspired men that the city would be taken and the sanctuary burnt to the ground by right of war, whensoever it should be united by sedition

113

and native hands should be the first to defile God's sacred precincts. This saying the Zealots did not disbelieve, yet they lent themselves as instruments to its accomplishment.

The Zealots and their allies in Jerusalem split into two factions. The Galileans gathered around John of Gischala. Others acknowledged the leadership of Eleazar, whom Josephus calls 'the most influential man of his sect'. By their capture of the Temple, the Zealots had come into possession of its great treasures. Fearing to lose them, they concealed the wealth in a number of places in and around Jerusalem. They devised clues for its recovery and inscribed these on a copper scroll which they hid in a cave in the cliff at Qumran, by the Dead Sea.

The discovery in 1952 of this Copper Scroll excited the curiosity of scholars, who concluded even before examination that this durable material had been chosen for some important purpose. The intricate task of unrolling the brittle copper sheets was accomplished in England, at the Manchester College of Technology. The deciphering of the text was undertaken by Mr John M. Allegro, at that time Lecturer in Old Testament Studies at Manchester University. He is a leading authority on the Scrolls, though others have differed with some of his writing.

There is no unanimity of opinion about the date when the various 'Dead Sea Scrolls' were written. It is generally agreed, however, that they were deposited in the caves at Qumran between A.D. 68 and 70, before the site was overrun by the Romans. To guard against theft, the Zealots disguised the clues to their caches in terms which could be understood only by the initiated. Skilled modern detective work was required to unravel these clues, cloaked by allusion to long past and forgotten events.

The wealth of the Temple was immense. The Jews had used its treasury as a private bank and each year its deposits were increased by the half-shekel poll tax paid by every Jew both within Palestine and throughout the Diaspora.

In addition to money, the Temple service required a profusion of vessels and ornaments made of silver and gold. The Copper Scroll enumerates fantastic treasures: 62 tons of silver, 26 tons of gold, 621 gold bars, 608 silver pitchers, 619 gold and silver vessels. According to Talmudic literature, a talent weighed 45 pounds; on that basis the treasure was valued at 3,282 talents of silver, and 1,280 talents of gold.

Allegro, in his book *The Treasure of the Copper Scroll*, has shown the absurdities of these values. If the talent weighed 45 pounds the two water pitchers listed in item 33 would have had to be capable between them of holding one and a half tons of liquid. The 'good and faithful servant' of the Parable of the Unjust Steward (*Matthew* 18:23–25) would have needed a wheelbarrow to bring his master four hundredweight of silver. The term 'talent', thinks Allegro, had ceased to be an exact monetary term and had become a slang word denoting the *maneh*, a coin of twelve ounces. His reasoning reduces the value of the treasure to 21¾ hundredweight of silver and 8½ hundredweight of gold, the equivalent in modern bullion of something in excess of £358,000 or $1,000,000.

The clues provided by the Copper Scroll indicate a number of sites. They are grouped in three areas: around the Dead Sea, in the region of Jericho, and in and around Jerusalem. To locate these sites now is difficult because of our ignorance of the everyday Jewish vocabulary of that time. Armed with the vocabulary of the Bible we could 'call the wrath of God upon an apostate city', but we would find it difficult to tell a gardener where to dig a ditch or dam a stream. And the Scroll is more concerned with ditches, streams, wells, cisterns, and underground passages than with man's failings. The word which the scribe used for 'reservoir' occurs in Hebrew literature only twice. The word for an underground passage is found only twice in the Bible. It has two contrary meanings: a tower and a hole in the ground. The scribe's cryptic meaning can only be guessed. Considerable knowledge of topography, ancient history, and long-forgotten place names is required to decipher the Scroll's message.

Take, for example, the first item of the Scroll, 'the Vale of Acor', in which stands the fortress where a money chest was hidden. No such name exists now. Drawing clues from obscure passages in ancient books, Allegro identifies the Vale of Acor as the valley which still leads from the Dead Sea towards Jerusalem. It lies only six miles from the ruins of an ancient fortification built by the Maccabees to protect the road to Jerusalem. The fort was reconstructed by Herod the Great. The ravages of time have destroyed the features referred to in the clue.

In another item, the scribe used the place-name 'Secach' to designate the buildings at Qumran. Its site fulfils the topographical description. 'Secach' probably meant a deep place or gorge. Josephus mentions such a place. There the Maccabean priest-king, Alexander Jannaeus (103–76 B.C.), 'pursued' the ringleaders of revolt. These appear to have been members of the Qumran community who had fallen foul of the 'Wicked Priest', which was probably their term for Alexander Jannaeus. At the 'Secach' the treasure had been concealed 'in the fissure of the plaster of Solomon's reservoir'. The word 'fissure' provides a further clue. It was used by the Jews of the time particularly to describe damage caused by an earthquake. A great earthquake struck the district in 31 B.C. Its effects can be seen to this day in the ruins at Qumran, where a great fissure, or crack, extends to 90 feet on the walls of the pool used for ritual ablutions. Here modern archaeologists would have to dig to a depth of four and a half feet.

Allegro adopts the same techniques of detection to identify other sites. The bulk of the treasure was hidden in and around Jerusalem. (Allegro's deciphering of the Copper Scroll has already contributed greatly to reconstruction of the ancient city.)

The layout of ancient Jerusalem has been learned from Josephus's description and from the remarkable work of three British army engineers: Captains Charles Wilson and Charles Warren and Corporal Birtles. In 1864 they explored the long-forgotten cisterns, tunnels, and underground passages that honeycomb the ground beneath the modern city. Their researches showed that ancient Jerusalem had been built upon two rocky spurs and was protected on its western, southern, and eastern sides by two deep valleys. It was also crossed by two shallow valleys intersecting at right angles. The ancient city was roughly divided into four sections: the south-eastern hill (site of the original Jebusite and Davidic cities), the south-

western hill, the north-western hill, and the rocky eminence at
the north-east. There successive Temples were built. The Antonia
fortress dominated the Temple precincts.

Between the Temple and the Mount of Olives lay two deep
valleys, named the Kidron and the Hinnom. The true name of
a third, south-to-north cross valley within the city requires
greater explanation. Its designation as the 'Tyropoeon' Valley in
the Greek text of Josephus is clearly a mistranslation from the
author's original Semitic. His translators misunderstood the
word he used for 'outer'. They believed it meant to congeal.
They interpreted it as 'cheese-making', calling it the Tyropoeon,
or the valley of the cheese-makers. When Josephus wrote, the
valley, though by then engulfed by the city, still retained its
ancient description as 'Outer'. Allegro's identification of clues
will bring us to this 'Outer Valley'.

The first item in the Copper Scroll takes us to the Antonia
fortress, which overlooked the Temple from the north. It refers
to the 'House of the Pools'. This is a thinly disguised identification of the twin pools or reservoirs which still lie beneath the
ruins of the fortress. But the scribe had no intention of making
the task easy. The site of the treasure is cloaked in vague terms,
familiar only to people who knew about these 'settling basins'.
Josephus provides the means by which this spot can be identified.

His Greek translators made another error when they interpreted his word for these 'settling basins' as a 'bird'. They
thought, perhaps, that he meant they were so shaped. (Josephus
in this passage is describing the Roman besiegers' stratagem for
raising a rampart against the wall of the fortress.) They were unaware that the Jews had tunnelled beneath them from the
ancient conduit which led to the settling basins. Its course was
found in 1864. The combination of clues indicates that the
treasure was concealed at the spot where the conduit entered
the settling basins. The basins still exist beneath the Convent
of the Sisters of Zion, where I inspected them.

Two further items indicate places in the Tyropoeon or Outer
Valley. To understand their significance we need to know more
about ancient Jerusalem. This valley was crossed by a bridge

(replacing a former dam), which connected the Citadel on the west to the Temple buildings on the east. By it stood the 'House of the High Priest'. The clue reads, 'In the Outer Valley, in the middle of the Circle-on-the-Stone, buried at seventeen cubits beneath it, 17 talents of silver and gold.'

This 'Circle-on-the-Stone', Allegro believes, meant a water-level gauge which lay on the floor of the Outer Valley beneath the original dam. Its name was derived from an ancient fable about a man named Onias, a famous rain-maker. He was called Onias the Circle-Maker because, when he forecast a much-needed downpour and it began to fall, the people rushed to see if the water would rise above the stone circle which formed the flood mark.

Another item in the Scroll's list of hiding places refers to the 'dam's sluice'. This may have been a conduit or tunnel leading from the dam. This sluice was found in 1864 by Wilson and Warren. They pursued it for 220 feet to the west, emerging finally in a stable, startling the owner. He rushed out swearing that he was followed by jinns. Modern archaeologists need only to measure 17 cubits (about 30 feet) below the Circle-on-the-Stone to rediscover the sluice or conduit where the seventeen and nine talents were hidden.

Two of the Scroll items required a visit to the Hinnom Valley. There the treasure was hidden in 'the stubble fields' and in the 'irrigation ditch' of the Shaveh. The word 'Shaveh' was employed to describe the plain at the Hinnom Valley's intersection with the Outer Valley. Wilson and Warren entered and crawled through this 700 foot tunnel which once carried water into the city. One treasure was hidden 36 feet from the entrance of the conduit and the other at its outlet.

Several of the Scroll treasures may have been concealed in the Kidron Valley. This part of the city has a peculiar significance for Christians. Here lay Gethsemane, the Garden of Agony, and perhaps even Golgotha itself, believes Allegro. The valley between the two hills—the Temple Mount and the Mount of Olives—fits the description of the place visible from afar which the Gospels failed to identify.

The clues to these treasure caches are derived partly from the

New Testament (which names the olive press at Gethsemane), and partly from Josephus. (He records that in the year A.D. 62 James, the brother of Jesus, was cast down from the pinnacle of the Temple, and stoned by his enemies.) The Pharisees called James the 'Just One'—the *Zaddik* or *Zadduk*. Such a name seems to have been given to a tomb which stood on the floor of the Kidron Valley. The Scroll says that a treasure had been hidden 'Below the Portico's southern corner, in the Tomb of Zadok, under the platform.' The Temple arcade, called the Portico, ran along its eastern side to the pinnacle at its south-eastern corner. The remnants of several tombs still exist in the valley at this spot, close to the 'grave of the common people', where other treasures were concealed.

Another treasure was hidden in the vat of the olive press. The scribe describes its plughole as being three and a half feet in width. Such a plughole exists still in the shallow troughs which can be seen on the hill above Zadok's tomb.

A number of concealments were made within the precincts of the Temple. It was a vast building. Several underground chambers and water cisterns remain, beneath the present Muslim Mosque. The scribe became very cautious about items concealed within the Temple. He disguised their locations by nicknames. Familiar though they may have been to the people who lived and worked in the Temple, these were unknown to outsiders. But modern knowledge of the source documents— Josephus and the Jewish *Mishnah* (a collection of rabbinic traditions)—enables the scholarly detective to identify some of these sixteen treasure sites.

Item 7 reads: 'In the cavity of the Old House of Tribute, in the Platform of the Chain: sixty-five bars of gold.'

According to the *Mishnah*, one of the most important buildings in the Inner Temple court was called the Chamber of the Fireplace, or Hearth. It contained a stone platform used as sleeping quarters by the duty watch of priests who were not actually on guard. The platform contained a stone slab which could be lifted by means of an iron ring. From the ring hung a chain; on it priests suspended the keys to the Temple's gates. This seems to be the place indicated in item 7, but why did the scribe call the chamber 'The House of Tribute'? This change of name, Allegro believes, resulted from the subterfuge adopted by Herod when he rebuilt the Temple. To create the building he desired without alienating the feelings of his Jewish subjects who disliked change, Herod called the reconstructed chamber by another name. If the Platform of the Chain can be found, the treasure seekers will need only to lift the stone slab to find sixty-five bars of gold in the cavity beneath.

It is unlikely that the Jews recovered their treasure. Most of the clues would have become obliterated after the destruction of Jerusalem in A.D. 70. Some caches may have been found by the Roman soldiers. Josephus records that they penetrated the subterranean tunnels in search of loot. Some may await discovery. In 1961 a small expedition financed by the London *Daily Mail* unearthed a jug containing silver coins at Qumran.

Thirteen

Vespasian's Advance

Josephus does not mention the concealment of the treasure. His knowledge of events within Jerusalem was scanty. About Roman affairs he wrote with greater authority, for he was a favoured prisoner in the camp. Whereas previously he had reported Vespasian's refusal to march on Jerusalem, he now shows that general determined to 'deliver it from siege'. Having finally subjugated Galilee, Vespasian determined to drive the remaining rebels into Jerusalem. Then, he would draw his noose tight around the city.

Vespasian advanced in the spring of A.D. 68 to isolate the rebel stronghold by a pincer movement. One part of his army headed southward across the Maritime Plain. Another pushed down the Jordan valley to Jericho. Vespasian visited the Dead Sea. To test its famous buoyancy, he ordered certain persons who were unable to swim to be flung into the deep water with their hands tied. 'All rose to the surface and floated, as if impelled by a current of air,' says Josephus. Leaving one legion at Jericho, Vespasian returned to Caesarea on the coast. He had subjugated the countryside around Jerusalem.

About this time, according to the tradition recorded by the Church historian Eusebius, the Christian community within Jerusalem—the Fathers of the Church—escaped from the doomed city. They made their way across the river Jordan and took refuge in the Gentile city of Pella, 60 miles to the northeast of Jerusalem. This story is incompatible with the facts.

Pella had been sacked and its citizens slaughtered by the Jews at the start of the revolt. Any Jews, however pacific, who sought asylum in Pella would, therefore, have suffered Gentile vengeance. There are other objections. If the Christians had attempted to leave Jerusalem they would have been killed as renegades. In their journey northwards they would have met the advancing Romans.

It seems probable that the Christians remained in Jerusalem sharing their countrymen's glorious cause. Like their friends the Zealots, they were buoyed up by hopes of divine deliverance.

The traditional picture of the early Christians as specific visionaries has so long conditioned our thinking that it is hard to visualize them as patriotic resistance fighters. But Jesus, we recall, had ordered his disciples to arm themselves. At Jesus's arrest, Peter offered armed resistance. He may later have murdered two people. It is difficult otherwise to explain the deaths of Ananias and Sapphira, a man and his wife. According to the record of *Acts*, they fell dead at Peter's feet within a matter of hours.

Their sudden deaths are attributed by the author of *Acts* to divine judgment. Luke explains that they had withheld part of the proceeds of the sale of a piece of property; all Christian property, however, was held in common.

Peter accused Ananias of lying to the Holy Spirit. Ananias fell down and died. The narrative continues: 'The young men rose and wrapped him and carried him out and buried him.' This was presumably a clandestine operation. Three hours later Sapphira comes, 'not knowing what had happened'. Peter accuses her also: 'How is it that you have agreed together to tempt the Spirit of the Lord?' He continues: 'Hark, the feet of those that have buried your husband are at the door and they will carry you out.' Sapphira immediately falls dead at Peter's feet and the young men dispose of her body. 'And a great fear came upon the whole church, and upon all those who heard of these things,' the author of *Acts* laconically records.

If the death of the husband had been natural or accidental, Peter should have been more careful with the wife. As the story stands it can only be assumed that Peter executed two members of the movement for a crime, the true nature of which is obscured. It is improbable that two adults could have died of fright, or accidentally, in Peter's presence.

Like the Zealots, the Jewish Christians hoped to establish the Kingdom of God. That perfect state could not be achieved until the Romans had been expelled from the Holy Land of Israel. The Christians believed that their dead Messiah would return to complete his mission, to restore the kingdom to Israel. As the Romans closed in around Jerusalem, they must have scanned the skies in expectation of his Second Coming.

One learned Pharisee succeeded in escaping from Jerusalem. Jonathan ben Zakkai, who ranked second only to Simon ben Gamaliel, deserted the city and went over to the Romans. He feigned death and was carried out on a bier. On reaching the Roman lines he saluted Vespasian as Emperor. Vespasian sent Jonathan to Jammia, near Joppa, where he established a school for the study of the law.

At Caesarea, Vespasian learned of the death of the Emperor Nero. The news led him to postpone his assault on Jerusalem. He needed to keep an observant eye on the confused state of affairs in Rome. Great issues were at stake, for the family of Caesars had become extinct. There was no obvious heir. The throne was seized first by Galba, who was murdered at the instigation of another general, Otho. In his turn Otho was overthrown by yet another general, Vitelius. His elevation infuriated Vespasian's soldiers. They acclaimed their own general as Emperor and swore allegiance to him. So did Tiberius Alexander, Governor of Egypt, and Mucianus, Legate of Syria. The Italian legions murdered Vitelius. In December, A.D. 69, Vespasian was acknowledged Emperor of Rome.

Vespasian, coming from Judaea, had become ruler of the inhabited world. Josephus's remarkable interpretation of the ancient oracle had come true. Releasing his prisoner, whom he named the 'Voice of God', Vespasian took ship to Rome. He left his son Titus to finish the Judaean campaign with Tiberius Alexander as his chief of staff and four legions. Josephus was raised to the rank of official historian.

Titus may have been favourably disposed towards the Jews. He had enjoyed a love affair with Agrippa II's sister, the princess Bernice, when she was already a middle-aged lady of unsavoury reputation. According to the Roman historian Suetonius, she had deserted her husband, Herod, King of Chalcis, for an incestuous union with her brother Agrippa. She abandoned

Agrippa in order to marry King Polemon of Cilicia. Later she returned to her brother. Her love affair with the twenty-seven-year-old Titus must have been short-lived. She accompanied Vespasian to Rome at the close of the year A.D. 69.

The new commander had won renown with his father in Germany and Britain. Suetonius states that Titus was 'naturally kind-hearted'. He seems to have displayed a conciliatory policy towards his defeated enemies.

In Jerusalem the civil war had taken a new turn. Alarmed by reports of the growing strength of Simon Gioras, the Jerusalem Zealots sallied out to attack him. They met with disaster and were driven back within their walls. Fearing to meet Simon again in open battle, they kidnapped his wife, hoping he would sue for her recovery. Instead, and 'raging like a wounded beast', he besieged Jerusalem. He sent messengers to inform the citizens that, unless his wife was restored, he would batter down the walls and kill every person within, irrespective of age or sex, innocence or guilt.

The remnants of the priestly party saw in Simon their last hope of safety. They opened the gates to Simon and he 'haughtily consented to be their despot'. Thus, states Josephus, in the third year of the war Simon became master of Jerusalem. In fact Simon only commanded the Upper City. John of Gischala's Galilean followers held the Temple precincts, while Eleazar and his Zealots occupied the Sanctuary. Simon fought to dislodge John, and John strove to oust Eleazar.

To win the Temple, Simon raised four huge towers outside and beneath its walls. On these he mounted the catapults and *ballistae* he had taken from the Twelfth Legion at Beth-horon. His archers and slingers rained missiles from below on the Temple's defenders, who were simultaneously assailed from above by Eleazar's javelins. Caught between two fires, John gained over Simon by his higher position. In this private war the buildings around the Temple were reduced to ashes. The fires destroyed the stores of corn which had been accumulated to endure for years.

The conflict in the Temple failed to deter the priests from performing the daily sacrifices. Many fell victims to the flying javelins, mingling their own blood with that of their sacrifices. (The *Talmud* records what may be a blurred echo of this conflict.) One priest stabbed another at the foot of the altar as they fought for precedence. Josephus described the scene:

> Old men and women in their helplessness prayed for the coming of the Romans and eagerly looked for the external war to liberate them from their internal miseries. Loyal citizens, for their part, were in dire despondency and alarm, having no opportunity for planning any change of policy, no hope of coming to terms or of flight, if they had the will; for watch was kept everywhere, and the brigand chiefs, divided on all else, put to death as their common enemies any in favour of peace with the Romans or suspected of an intention to desert, and were unanimous only in slaughtering those deserving of deliverance.

By day and by night the shouts of the combatants rang incessantly, drowning even the terrified lamentations of the mourners. Trampling over dead bodies, leaving untried no outrage or brutality, the warring partisans strove for the mastery of Jerusalem.

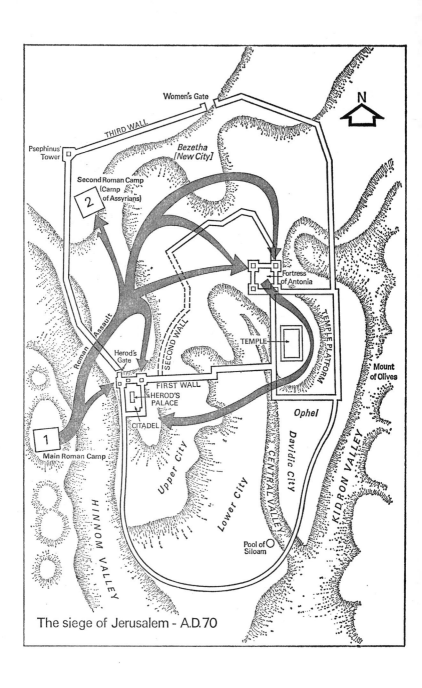

The siege of Jerusalem - A.D. 70

Fourteen

The Walls
of Jerusalem

On the hills surrounding Jerusalem glinted the Roman armour. Titus, marching from Caesarea with two legions—the Twelfth and Fifteenth—ascended the Judaean hills, passed through the Beth-horons, turned south on to the highroad from the north, and encamped at Saul's Hill, a village about four miles from Jerusalem. The Tenth Legion came from Jericho, and the Fifth from Emmaus. Leaving his army to fortify the camp, Titus and his officers rode forward to reconnoitre the city's strength. He wanted to 'test the mettle of the Jews' and to learn whether, upon seeing the Romans, they would be terrified into surrender. Riding ahead of his bodyguard, Titus drew rein on Mount Scopus. Spread out below him, three-quarters of a mile distant, lay Jerusalem, its white buildings gleaming in the spring sunshine.

In 1969, from a position equivalent to Mount Scopus (the 'lookout place'), I gazed upon exactly the same scene. Any tourist can do the same by visiting the model of the ancient city at the Holy Land Hotel. This unique model was built by the hotel owner, Mr Hans Krock, in memory of his son killed in the 1948 war. The archaeological and topographical data was supplied by Professor M. Avi-Yonah, of the Hebrew University, who showed me round. Next day he accompanied me through the ancient city itself, on the first of my several visits of inspection.

Despite its almost total destruction in A.D. 70, and the inevitable changes that have occurred in nineteen centuries, the city's overall outline on the east, south, and west is not very different from that upon which Titus gazed. The three dominant features, the Temple, the Antonia fortress, and Herod's palace, have disappeared, and the northern defensive wall exists only in fragments.

As a dwelling place Jerusalem owed its origin to its defensive qualities. The site offered no other advantages. It neither dominated communications nor was surrounded by fertile land. The countryside is waterless. That factor made Jerusalem hard to capture. Its defenders could draw upon the water they had stored in cisterns; the besiegers were forced to search far afield to replenish their supplies. We need to go down to the basic contours to understand the strength of the ancient city and its defences.

The site of Jerusalem is usually described as formed of two spurs. They project southwards from the northern watershed-ridge, and descend into the valleys of Kidron and Hinnom. These valleys in their turn, are surrounded by ridges higher than that from which Jerusalem projects. It is easier, perhaps, to visualize the site in terms of three spurs. They project like the first three fingers of a hand turned palm uppermost. The palm with its 'humps and hollows' represents the watershed-ridge. The three fingers, the middle one for our purposes being shorter than the others, indicate the three spurs: the south-eastern hill, the shorter central ridge, and the south-western hill. They protrude above the three-hundred-foot-deep and precipitous ravines by which the city is surrounded on three sides.

Another, shallower valley, the Central or 'Outer' (Tyropoeon) Valley, as it was called because it lay outside the original city, intersected the centre of the ancient city running from south to north. A smaller depression to the west raised the central ridge between the two chief spurs, the south-eastern and south-western hills.

At the base of these spurs (at the base of the fingers) ran a cross-ravine which, with the central valley, isolated the two chief promontories: the summit of the south-eastern hill (2,440 feet) and the summit of the south-western spur (2,581 feet). On them stood the city's two strong points: the Temple and Herod's palace, sometimes called the Citadel.

The third strong point, the Antonia fortress, stood on the

narrow saddle (2,462 feet) at the north-western corner of the Temple platform. That area, 800 by 300 feet, had been formed by flattening the summit of the south-eastern hill. There Solomon had built his palace and temple. The size of this platform was considerably enlarged by Herod, who built strong sustaining walls which enclosed the slopes of the hill. He also reconstructed the ancient fortress on the north-west, re-naming it in honour of Anthony, Cleopatra's lover. Leaving for a moment a more detailed description of the Temple and the Antonia, we can look at the rest of the city as it stood in A.D. 70.

As their population increased, the Jews progressively extended the city from the small Jebusite–Davidic town which had been built on the slopes of the south-eastern hill. This became known as 'Ophel'. In time it extended across the Central Valley, westwards and up the slopes of the south-western hill. These additions were named the Lower and Upper Cities. The latter was in time dominated by the bastions of Herod's palace on the north-western crest of that ridge.

To enclose the city from the north the Jews built a wall—the 'First Wall', as it is called—from the Citadel to the Temple. The course of the wall, and its encirclement of the southern sections of the city, is not disputed, for it followed the natural contour line, from near the modern Jaffa Gate, along the modern David Street and the Street of the Chain, to the western wall of the Temple. The southern section of this First Wall was not involved in the Roman siege. It enclosed the Pool of Siloam, at the base of the south-eastern hill.

When the Jews needed to expand the city to the north, they built the Second Wall—some time before 37 B.C., for Josephus describes it as covering the northern front of the city from the western hill to the Antonia.

The line of this Second Wall is uncertain. 'An attempt to solve the problem of the Second Wall,' remarks Professor Avi-Yonah (*Israel Exploration Society Journal*, Vol. 18, No. 2) 'must begin by positioning the Third.' He means the wall begun by King Agrippa I to enclose Bezetha, the New City.

The evidence for the determination of these walls falls into three categories; archaeological, topographical, and historical.

Josephus is our only historical source and his description is hopelessly muddled. From it one useful fact emerges.

Agrippa began but did not finish the Third Wall. It was completed about A.D. 67 by the insurgents. That the so-called 'Agrippa's Wall' did not exist before A.D. 67 is a point of considerable importance. The discovery of coins dated between A.D. 54 and 59 at a site excavated in 1926 proves that one section had not then been built.

Part of the Third Wall, a line of massive stones extending over a distance of some 417 yards, has been unearthed o·6 miles north of the city. They follow the line of the 765-metre (about 836-yard) contour, exactly the line along that ridge which, for strategic reasons, would have been chosen for such a defensive wall. E. L. Sukenik and L. A. Mayer (in *The Third Wall of Jerusalem*) have observed that 'anyone wanting to enclose the town with a wall from this side could not have chosen a more suitable site'. Any line which did not extend thus far to the north, remarks Avi-Yonah, would have been 'strategically unsound'.

The identification of this line of stones as the long-lost Third Wall is not accepted by Dr Kathleen Kenyon (*Jerusalem : Excavating 3,000 Years of History*). She claims that they comprise the remnants of the siege wall with which the Romans encompassed the city. She believes that the present 'Turkish Wall' represents the line of the Third Wall.

Sections of the wall discovered on the 765-metre contour can be seen at various points on Richard Coeur-de-Lion Street where it crosses the Nablus road (the highway to the north from the Damascus Gate). I inspected several sections which lie to the south of St George's Cathedral, and along the ridge of the 765-metre contour.

On one point there is no clash of opinion. The Third Wall started on the west from Herod's bastions, and on the east from the north-eastern corner of the Temple platform. How far these western and eastern walls extended to the north depends on the position of the Psephinus tower which was constructed at the north-western corner of the wall. Here Josephus can help us. He says that from the platform of this tower, on a clear day, it was possible to see both the Nabataean hills east of the Dead Sea, and the sea coast of the Mediterranean. The tower rose to the height of 70 cubits, or about 115 feet. Such an unobstructed view above the Mount of Olives (880 yards) to the east and the Romema hill (905 yards) to the west, could have been obtained from a tower of that height only if it stood at an elevation of 873 yards. That height is reached near the bend of Prophets' Street, and significantly near the ancient quarry. Even more significant, the place where the Psephinus tower must have stood lies on the direct east-west line of the stones discovered in 1925.

The course of events provides further clues. Titus breached the Third Wall from the west on May 25. Following his success, he shifted his camp to within the Third Wall. He selected the site known as the Camp of the Assyrians. This was 'out of bow-shot', or some 200 yards distant from the Second Wall. Five days later he captured the Second Wall and built his own wall around the whole city, an operation which was completed in three days. Josephus's statements support the identification of the line of stones discovered on the 765-metre contour with the Third Wall. If that wall is now represented by the Turkish Wall, it means that Titus ran his siege wall *behind* his new camp, which had no parallel in Roman siege tactics. Such a line of construction would have failed in its objectives: to prevent the Jews from escaping the doomed city and from attacking the Roman camp. No siege wall run on such a line, due to its far greater length, could have been completed in three days.

Professor Avi-Yonah's reasoning is confirmed by the lie of the land. The Third Wall was to the north of the present Turkish Wall, one section of which may have formed part of the Second Wall. This, according to Josephus, 'started (on the west) from the gate in the First Wall, which was called Gennath, and encircled only the slope towards the north and went up as far as the Antonia'. It was short and contained only fourteen towers, as against sixty on the First Wall and ninety on the Third Wall. It was relatively weak, for Titus stormed it in five days. While the site of the gate Gennath is unknown, its name 'the Gate of the Gardens' implies that it stood at the western end of the First Wall. The archaeological evidence is of little help in establishing the course of the Second Wall; Herodian stonework has been found beneath the Damascus Gate, and portions of a very early wall have been unearthed within the Old City, on a rock scarp north of David Street, at about the spot where the Second Wall may have turned northwards from the First Wall.

Starting from this point, the Second Wall probably ran along the 765-metre (825-yard) contour. It encircled the northern end of the Central Valley, followed the line of the later Turkish Wall from the Damascus Gate to Herod's Gate, and turned southwards in a semi-circle along the saddle on which stood the Antonia, which it reached at its north-eastern corner. The western section of the Second Wall cannot be determined with certainty.

All three walls probably rose to the height of 20 feet. They were protected by battlements and intersected by towers. My plan, which is based on E. F. Beaumont's relief map, indicates the probable line of the city's walls on which Titus gazed in April, A.D. 70.

One point requires emphasis. Jerusalem could be assailed only from the north and north-west. On all other sides it was surrounded by deep valleys.

Fifteen

Breaching
the Third Wall

Titus halted on Mount Scopus. Seeing no Jews on the walls, he and his staff rode down the slope, followed by a bodyguard of six hundred horsemen, to reconnoitre the city. The cavalry lagged behind. Suddenly from the 'Women's Gate' in the outer wall dashed an immense number of Jews. They broke through the cavalry, preventing them from following Titus. The horsemen retreated, unaware of the peril in which their general stood. The ground Titus and his bodyguard had reached was 'all cut up by trenches for gardening purposes and intersected by cross-walls and numbers of fences'. These obstacles impeded his escape. The only way to safety lay through the Jews. Titus led his officers in a charge which cut through the enemy. Several of his men were dismounted and speared by the Jews, who returned to the city elated by their success.

Next day, Titus moved two legions to Mount Scopus. The Tenth Legion, marching from Jericho, reached the Mount of Olives, where it set to work building a camp.

Within Jerusalem the three factions suspended their private war temporarily, in order to resist the threat from without. Banding together, the patriots sallied out from the eastern and southern ramparts, raced across the Kidron Valley, climbed the slopes of the Mount of Olives and attacked the Tenth Legion. The Romans were taken unawares. Thrown into disorder by the unexpected sally, the legionaries retreated before the Jewish onrush. They were saved from complete rout only by the timely intervention of Titus. Rallying the fugitives, Titus drove the Jews headlong down the ravine and across the brook. Satisfied that he had saved the situation, he returned to the upper slopes of the Mount, deploying his soldiers to protect the legionaries as they completed their fortifications. The Jews, who had been reinforced, recrossed the brook and sprang up the slopes—'with such impetuosity that their rush was comparable to that of the most savage of beasts', says Josephus. He may have witnessed the skirmish. Again the Romans broke ranks and fled, leaving their general and a few men to face the attack of their enemy—who seemed to court death, so fierce was their onslaught. Titus led another counterattack, driving the Jews once again across the Kidron.

Following his rescue of the Tenth Legion, Titus broke camp and marched his two legions from Mount Scopus around to the west of Jerusalem. There he was joined by the Fifth Legion, which had climbed the hills from Emmaus. These three legions, with the Tenth from the Mount of Olives, spread out to complete the encirclement of the city. Titus debated the situation with his officers. He could either starve out the Jews or storm the city. Both plans offered advantages. Torn by internal dissension and lacking supplies, the Jews would be unable to withstand a long siege. Compelling reasons demanded a quick Roman victory. The soldiers, stated Tacitus, clamoured to be led in a direct assault. It was, they declared, beneath their dignity 'to starve out such a rabble'. Titus, too, was anxious to win a notable success in order to give prestige to the new dynasty. And he desired, says the historian Tacitus, to return to Rome, to 'enjoy its delights'.

Titus must have listened to the advice of his chief of staff, Tiberius Alexander. As a former Procurator of Judaea, Tiberius would have been familiar with the defences of Jerusalem. All previous besiegers, including the Roman general Pompey, had assaulted the city from the north. Casting aside precedent, Titus decided to breach the outer or Third Wall from the north-west. He planned to capture Jerusalem quickly in one terrific blow, by launching simultaneous assaults on the Antonia fortress and the royal palace. First he needed to break down the Third Wall.

Titus underestimated the strength of Jerusalem and the fanatical determination of its defenders. They were prepared to die for God's Holy Sanctuary. But they were still reluctant to unite against the common foe.

Seizing the opportunity provided by the Passover, John of Gischala infiltrated his troops into the Temple with the worshippers. Once within the sacred precincts, they cast aside their disguise and drew their weapons, and routed Eleazar's men, who took refuge in the vaults. The two leaders, Zealot and Galilean, agreed to merge their forces, Eleazar's 2,400 men with John's 5,000. Thus John gained control of both the Temple and the Antonia fortress. The Upper and Lower Cities, with Herod's palace, remained in the hands of Simon Gioras. According to Josephus he led a mixed force of Zealots and Idumaeans numbering about 15,000 men.

The population of the city was swollen with refugees from the countryside and by the pilgrims who still came for the Passover. Within it lurked the survivors of the Jewish peace-party. Their gloomy predictions frightened many citizens. On the approach of the Romans, says Tacitus, 'contending hosts were seen marching in the skies, arms flashed, and suddenly the Temple was illuminated with fire from the clouds. Of a sudden the doors of the Shrine opened and a super human voice cried "the gods are departing", and at the same moment the mighty stir of their going was heard.'

The Jews were still divided in their aims. 'Not even when the Romans encamped beneath the walls, did the civil strife slacken within,' recorded Josephus. Following each sally, the parties fell to fighting again.

Simon Gioras contrived to trick the Romans. A band of men emerged from a gate and appeared to flee, as if they had been ejected by the other party. They pretended equal terror of the Romans, cowering together in a bunch. Their comrades, lining the walls, shouted 'Peace! Peace!' and clamoured for protection. Showering stones on their own men, they promised the Romans to open the city gates. The first party kept up the deception by alternately running back to re-enter the gate, clamouring to be admitted, and rushing towards the Romans with every sign of agitation and fear. Believing that the peace party were ready to open the gates, many of the Roman soldiers became excited and were only stopped by Titus from rushing the gate. He viewed 'this surprising invitation with suspicion', for only the day before he had sent Josephus to offer terms which had been rejected. Many venturesome soldiers disobeyed orders. They ran towards the gate, through the open portals of which the decoys retired. Simon's troops allowed their dupes to reach the wall before they showered down volleys of stones and missiles, killing and wounding many. The decoys turned back to attack the astonished soldiers. Ashamed of their error and dreading its consequences, the Romans persevered in their blunder. Finally, driven back by weight of numbers, they retired ignominiously, pursued by the Jews, who, jeering and dancing for joy, retired only when the fugitives reached their own lines.

Titus was furiously angry. Calling together the rash adventurers, he lashed them with sarcasm, contrasting their lack of discipline and intemperate pugnacity with the wily forethought of their enemy. The Jews, he said, did everything with circumspection, carefully planning their stratagems and ambuscades. He dreaded to think, he told the crestfallen soldiers, what his father would say when he heard of such disobedience. He reminded them that among Romans 'even a victory without orders is held dishonourable'. The offenders gave themselves up for lost. They expected instant execution. But the other legionaries entreated leniency for their reckless comrades. Titus yielded. He was constrained, says Josephus, by considerations of expediency, for a great number of men were involved. He admonished the offenders and advised them to be wiser in future, reflecting privately as to how he might be avenged on the Jews.

To prevent further sallies from the city, Titus drew up the legions in martial array, infantry in front, cavalry behind, each marshalled in three ranks, with the archers in the centre to protect the workmen and the transport drivers engaged in shifting and building camps. Titus himself encamped temporarily near the Psephinus Tower. Later he moved his main camp to a site on the west side of the city, probably that now occupied by the King David Hotel. While the legionaries were occupied fortifying their camps, Titus and his staff rode around the walls. He selected the spot at which to breach the Third Wall. Josephus describes it as 'opposite the tomb of John the High-

Priest', or John Hyrcanus (135–105 B.C.). (The site of the tomb is no longer identifiable.)

Titus probably chose to assail the western side of the Third Wall, the section which lay immediately to the north of the present Jaffa Gate. First he set his men to work levelling the ground up to the wall. Every fence and palisade with which the inhabitants of Jerusalem had enclosed their gardens was swept away. Every tree was felled. The cavities were filled in, the projecting rocks demolished. To collect timber with which to construct their siege engines, the soldiers stripped the city's environs of trees. The slope of the ground aided the work, otherwise hindered by the vigilance of the Jews. When Titus and his staff rode forward the enemy loosed a flight of arrows. One wounded the Tribune Nicanor. Convinced now of the Jews' animosity, Titus gave orders to commence the assault. He formed his army into three divisions, placing the artillery strategically to check any attempt by the defenders to impede the advance of the siege towers.

The sight of these preparations gave heart to those within the city who hoped, says Josephus, to gain respite while their oppressors were engaged in repelling the external foe. Even this new onslaught failed to unify the defenders. John did not stir to help Simon, who commanded the walls threatened by the Roman assault.

Simon placed his artillery on the walls. His men, though inexperienced in their use, fired missiles at the siege engines. To protect them the Romans erected palisades. They repelled the frequent Jewish sorties with missiles fired from their own artillery. These, says Josephus, were wonderfully constructed, particularly those belonging to the Tenth Legion:

Their quick-firers were more powerful and their stone-projectors larger, enabling them to repel not only the sallying parties but also those on the ramparts. The rocks which they hurled weighed a talent and had a range of two furlongs or more; and their impact not only to those who first met it but even to those considerably in the rear was irresistible.

By estimating the weight of those stone balls at a talent, Josephus implies that they weighed about half a hundredweight. Modern research has disclosed that stones propelled by these torsion catapults had an effective range of about 400 yards. The arrows fired from the *ballistae* flew nearly 500 yards. Since these are extreme ranges, the engines were probably effective only up to about half those distances. Both weapons were calibrated. E. W. Marsden (*Greek and Roman Artillery*) states 'there is good reason to believe that ancient artillery was extremely accurate'. The Roman engineers, Josephus explains, measured the distance from the walls by lead and line to gauge where to place their artillery. Their missiles were employed chiefly against personnel—at 400 yards a stone shot could plough through several ranks of soldiers. During the siege they were employed by the Romans chiefly to immobilize the defenders on the walls. Those in their turn shot flaming missiles in an attempt to set fire to the Roman siege towers.

The Jews learned quickly how to guard against the stones which flew above the walls. Being white in colour they could be detected by the eye as well as by the whizzing sound they made as they flew through the air. Watchmen posted on the walls gave warning when an engine was fired. Spotting the projectile in mid-air they shouted, 'Stone's coming!' pointing in its direction. Whereupon those who stood in line of fire fell to the ground, allowing the missile to fly harmlessly above their heads. The Romans then blackened the shot, making it more difficult to detect.

A stone struck off the head of that Jesus whose prophecies of disaster had disturbed the Jews before the start of the revolt. Though continuously under galling fire, the Jews, states Josephus, did not suffer the Romans to raise their siege works unmolested. They strove day and night by every resource of ingenuity and daring to hinder their construction.

The Romans pushed three siege towers against the walls. These mobile towers, the front and sides of which were protected by iron plates, contained three compartments. The bottom one was filled with men who pushed the tower forward along the levelled ground. The first floor contained arrow-throwing catapults and fire appliances. The second and top floors reached above the walls. In these were placed the slingers and archers. Their duty was to immobilize the defenders and to prevent them from interfering with the working of the battering ram. This was a heavy, iron-tipped baulk of timber. Suspended from the sides of the tower, it swung backwards and forwards, pounding the wall. The ram could be drawn up or lowered to strike the wall at its weakest point, somewhere above its solid base. Only two methods of defence were effective against these towers: to turn them over or to set them on fire with flaming missiles.

The battering of these rams raised a terrific din. It aroused the Jews to their common danger, forcing the rival factions to unite. Simon invited John to send his men to help defend the north wall. John, though mistrustful, gave permission for his soldiers to leave the Temple. Suspending temporarily their private war, the Jews massed on the Third Wall. They lined its ramparts and hurled stones and firebrands at the Roman siege engines, keeping them under incessant fire.

> The more venturesome, dashing out in bands, tore up the hurdles protecting the machines, and, falling upon the gunners, seldom through skill but generally through intrepidity, got the better of them. Titus, however, invariably came in person to the relief of those who were hard pressed, and posting his horses and archers on either side of the engines, kept the incendiaries at bay, beat back assailants from the towers, and brought the battering rams into action. For all that, the wall did not succumb to the blows, save the ram of the XVth legion dislodged the corner of a tower, but the wall itself was unimpaired, for it was not involved in immediate danger along with the tower, which projected far out and so could not easily bring down with it any of the main rampart.

Incautiously, Titus withdrew the protecting cavalry. Seizing their opportunity, a band of Zealots dashed out from a concealed gate near the Hippicus Tower, one of the bastions of Herod's palace. They carried the firebrands with which to burn the siege towers. They easily routed the first Romans they encountered. Pressing on they reached one of the machines, the wooden walls of which they set alight. Titus, hearing the sounds of combat, brought up his cavalry. He charged and dispersed the Jews, performing, according to Josephus, prodigies of personal valour. The flames having been extinguished, Titus ordered a Jewish prisoner to be crucified in sight of his comrades, hoping thereby to intimidate them. More serious to the Jews was the loss of one of their most gallant commanders. The breast of the Idumaean chieftain John was transfixed by an arrow.

The assault on the Third Wall continued for fifteen days. The Roman rams battered the walls while Roman artillery kept up an incessant fire, forcing the defenders to abandon their ramparts. So violent were the Roman volleys that the Jews named one of these siege engines, which belonged to the Tenth Legion, 'Victor', a tribute to its vanquishing of all obstacles. This engine threw very heavy stones, shaking the walls on impact. Under steady battering they began to crumble. At last, on May 25, the Romans succeeded in breaching the wall. They scaled it and opened its gates, through which the soldiers surged. The Jews retreated to their Second Wall. Titus shifted his camp within the Outer Wall, occupying the site known as the Camp of the Assyrians because the soldiers of Sennacherib had encamped there in 721 B.C.

Sixteen

The Assault on
the Second Wall

The Romans had achieved their first objective. Ahead stood the far stronger Second Wall. At its north-eastern corner rose the Antonia fortress, key to the city. Its position on the saddle between the Kidron and Central valleys made it unassailable until the Second Wall had been stormed.

Josephus does not indicate the spot where Titus assaulted the Second Wall. He states only that one battering ram was brought against the 'Central Tower of the North Wall.' This suggests that Titus concentrated his attack on the section of that wall which protected the head of the Central Valley, the direct approach to the Antonia. Divining Titus's purpose, the Jews massed upon the ramparts. John's division defended the Antonia. Simon's troops manned the whole course of the Second Wall, part of the First Wall (where it joined the Second Wall), and the bastions of Herod's palace. The Jews were not content with defending their walls. They dashed out, engaging the Romans in hand-to-hand fighting, only to be driven back within their walls—'through lack of the Romans' military skill', says Josephus. But they excelled themselves when fighting from their ramparts. There they were sustained by their daring and by their fortitude in face of calamity. 'Moreover they still cherished hopes of salvation,' adds the hostile historian, who did after all understand the religious motivation of the defenders who awaited a saving miracle from God.

Neither army felt fatigue. Hostilities continued without let-up from daylight to dusk. No form of warfare was omitted. Darkness scarcely brought respite, for both armies spent the night under arms. Anxiety made night more terrible than day. One party dreaded every moment the capture of the wall; the other feared invasion of their camp. Fighting resumed at dawn.

Each Jew strove to be foremost in the fray. Seeking a base motive to account for the courage of the defenders, Josephus claims they strove to win favour with their officers. Among these, Simon Gioras, he says, was regarded with 'reverence and awe'. Such was the esteem in which he was held that the men he commanded were prepared to take their own lives, should he give the order. (This is a striking admission of the standing of Simon, whom Josephus usually prefers to call a brigand.)

The Roman incentive to valour came from habit of victory and their inexperience of defeat. The personal example of Titus sometimes led to dangerous emulation. One day the Jews and Romans were engaged in combat outside the walls, each side throwing javelins from a distance. A Roman trooper named Longinus leaped from the lines and dashed into the middle of the Jews. He broke their ranks, killing two with his javelin, before escaping unscathed. His action, the gallantry of which was admitted, drew Titus's disapproval. 'Valour,' he said, 'only deserves the name when coupled with forethought and regard for security.' He ordered his soldiers to prove their manhood without running personal risks. The valour of the Jews was of a different order. 'Death seemed to them a trivial matter if it involved the fall of one of the enemy,' states the eyewitness.

A man named Castor employed a ruse to delay the fall of the Central Tower, as it rocked under the blows of the rams. Routed by Roman arrows, the other defenders of the wall had retreated. Castor and ten of his comrades hid below the ramparts. Suddenly they rose, stretching out their hands in supplication and imploring Titus to spare them. Believing that the Jews were at length relenting, he halted the battering, forbade the archers to shoot, and invited Castor to state what he wanted. He agreed to come down under pledge of protection. Titus offered security, whereupon the ten Jews fell to wrangling, five joining Castor in his fervent supplications and five crying that they would rather die than become slaves. Castor urged his recalcitrant comrades to accept the offered pledge. The assault along the whole wall became suspended while the Jews argued. Simulating battle, they brandished their swords and clashed their breastplates; some fell down in feigned death. Titus could not see exactly what was going on. The excitement proved too much for one Roman archer. Disobeying orders, he loosed an arrow which struck Castor in the nose.

Castor drew out the arrow, feigning indignation. He complained that he had been unfairly treated. Titus sternly rebuked the archer and ordered Josephus to talk with Castor. Josephus had, of course, seen through the ruse from the start. He declined to parley with Castor. A Jewish deserter named Aeneas ran to the wall. Castor said he wished to bring his money with him. Aeneas spread out his cloak to receive it. Instead of money Castor hurled a stone. It missed Aeneas but struck and wounded a soldier. Titus, indignant at Castor's mockery, ordered the battering ram to be set to work more vigorously than before. The tower collapsed under the blows. Castor set fire to it, and he and his friends leaped into the vault below, plunging into the fire rather than surrender.

On May 30, the fifth day of the assault, part of the Second Wall collapsed. The Jews retreated to the First Wall. Titus, states Josephus, offered the defenders the opportunity to descend from their wall and fight in the open. To those who wished for peace, he promised restoration of their property. The Jewish fighters threatened to kill all those who attempted to surrender or even talked of peace. They declared that Titus made such overtures because of his inability to capture the city. The excited legionaries climbed the debris of the Second Wall, failing to widen the breach, and rushed through the tortuous alleys between it and the First Wall. Opening their gates, the Jews sallied out, trapping the Romans within the narrow streets. Some Jews threw missiles from the rooftops; others issued from more distant gates. They drove the Romans back to the Second Wall. The breach was too narrow for them to retire together, and the Romans stood encircled by an ever-increasing ring of enemies. Titus came to their rescue. According to Josephus, he threw himself into the fray, holding back the Jews until all his soldiers had retired through the breach.

The Jews regained possession of the Second Wall. This feat elated the war party. They believed that the Romans would never venture again into the city. If they did, its defenders would again prove invincible. God, remarks Josephus, blinded their minds. They perceived neither that they were far outnumbered nor that famine would soon be upon them. The Jews retained possession of the Second Wall for only three days. Unable to withstand the renewed Roman assault, they retreated to the First Wall. Titus laid waste the intervening area.

Titus suspended the siege. To overawe the Jews he paraded his whole army in full sight of the walls, hoping that this display of Roman might would induce the Jews to surrender. He sent Josephus to parley. Keeping out of range of missiles, yet approaching to within earshot (a remarkable feat which he leaves unexplained), Josephus exorted the Jews to surrender. He told them that the might of Rome was irresistible—God was on the Roman side. 'Yield to the stronger,' he urged. The Romans, he declared, would bear no malice for the past and were lenient in victory. The exhortation was simple and direct. The Jews had triumphed in the past because they had fought in God's cause. By their iniquities and impieties they had lost God's help.

His words induced many Jews to desert. The rich swallowed their gold coins. After reaching the Roman lines, they were observed picking gold coins from their excrement. This sight, says Josephus, aroused the greed of the Syrian auxiliaries, who waylaid the deserters, ripping open their stomachs and searching the intestines. Titus was indignant when he heard of this atrocity. He decreed death for it in the future. But he was too late to save the 'two thousand victims who thus perished'. From then on the search for coins was conducted furtively.

The story is told in the *Mishnah* that some inhabitants lowered from the walls baskets containing gold in exchange for baskets of food. The traffic did not last long; the Romans filled the baskets with straw. To tantalize the defenders, the Romans roasted goats under the walls. The appetizing smell made the now starving people delirious.

As the siege became more severe the insurgents sought everywhere for food. They broke into houses, snatching morsels from the inmates' very jaws, torturing them to disclose their secret hiding places. So fearful became the citizens that they retired to the inner recesses of their houses to eat what food they had, thereby inducing the fate they had hoped to avoid. Seeing the houses shut up, the predatory bands assumed that food was being secretly consumed and broke in. In their fear, states Josephus, wives snatched food from husbands, children from fathers, and mothers from their infants' mouths. One mother, a woman of good family, named Mary, weary of finding food, slew, roasted and ate her own baby. She offered the remnants of the little carcass to the executioners who, scenting the odour, had burst into the house. Another woman, the pampered widow of the ex-High Priest Jonathan (her story is told in the *Mishnah*), was unable to buy food with her very considerable widow's maintenance and threw her worthless gold into the street.

Famished mourners fell dead while burying their friends. Hunger so stifled their emotions that there was neither wailing nor lamentations; 'with dry eyes and grinning mouths the dying victims looked on those who had gone to their rest before them'.

The city, wrapped in profound silence and night laden with death, was in the grip of a yet fiercer foe—the brigands. For breaking into habitations that were now mere charnal-houses, they rifled the dead and stripped the coverings from the bodies departed with shouts of laughter; they tried the points of their swords on the corpses and ran them through some of the prostrate but still living wretches, to test the temper of the blade, but any who implored them to lend them their hand and sword they disdainfully left to the mercy of the famine. And each victim expired with his eyes fixed on the Temple and averted from the rebels whom he left alive. The latter at the outset ordered the bodies to be buried at the public expense, finding the stench intolerable; afterwards, when incapable of continuing that, they flung them from the ramparts into the ravine.

At night scavengers crept into the ravines around the city to gather herbs. On their return they were seized and searched by the insurgents, who reaped the reward of reckless endeavour. Those captured by the Romans were scourged and crucified within sight of the walls. So great became their number that space could not be found for the crosses, or crosses for their bodies. Titus did not wish to deter true deserters. He ordered that prisoners should have their hands amputated and be sent back to the city. Five hundred deserters were captured daily, states Josephus. He was personally involved in the fate of the wretched citizens; his mother and father were held captive within the city by the war party.

Personal anxiety, if such a human feeling can be attributed to the callous Josephus, failed to diminish his zeal. He kept an observant eye for detail. He records the exploit of the youthful chieftain Antiochus Epiphanes, son of King Antiochus IV of Commagene. He had joined the Romans, bringing a bodyguard of young firebrands who called themselves 'Macedonians' in emulation of the famous Alexander. Antiochus expressed to Titus his surprise that the Romans hesitated to attack the city's ramparts. Titus told him with a smile, 'The field is yours.' Without further ado, the daring young man rushed at the wall. His comrades, lacking his skill, quickly fell victim to the hail of missiles poured upon them. Wounded and overpowered they retired, reflecting, remarks Josephus, that 'even genuine Macedonians, if they are to conquer, must have Alexander's fortune'.

Commenting on this stage of the siege, now in its second month, Josephus praised its defenders. They were prepared to die to the last man to save the Holy City from heathen desecration. His tribute is the more valuable because it is grudging.

Seventeen

The Antonia—
Key to the City

After fifteen days of continuous toil, the Romans stood ready
to launch their final assault. To bring their siege towers into
position they had built four immense earthern ramparts against
the wall. As usual, Josephus is hazy about where these ramparts were built. The positions of two are clear. The Fifth
Legion raised its earthwork against the north-western tower of
the Antonia. The Twelfth Legion built theirs about thirty feet
away. While we cannot exactly identify the locations of the
others, Josephus's vague description provides a clue to Titus's
intentions. The Tenth Legion raised their embankment 'at a
considerable distance from these', in 'the northern region' near
the pool named Amygdalon. This had been identified as the
'Pool of the Patriarch's Bath', which lay between the modern
Jaffa Gate and the Church of the Holy Sepulchre. The embankment was thus raised at the place where the First and Second
walls joined. The Fifteenth raised its bank opposite the High
Priest's Monument, which means that it intended to assault
the First Wall, somewhere near the modern Jaffa Gate.

These dispositions indicate that Titus intended to make two
simultaneous assaults. One would be directed against the Antonia fortress, the other against the western corner of the First
Wall. He hoped to win the city by one decisive blow. The
Temple was the objective. If both assaults succeeded, he would
be able to storm the Sanctuary from both sides, from the Antonia on the north and from the Upper City on the west.

The strength of the Antonia was prodigious. It comprised
four square towers, one at each corner. The south-eastern tower
rose to 115 feet and was higher than the others. The fortress
was protected on the north by a moat 'which made the elevation
of the towers more remarkable', and it stood on the saddle be-

tween two valleys, which made access difficult. It dominated
the Temple, to which it was connected by staircases.

In 63 B.C. the Roman general Pompey had found the previous fortress on the site a hard nut to crack. The geographer-
historian Strabo says that this earlier Hasmonaean fort, named
the Baris, was protected on the north by a ditch 60 feet deep
and 250 feet broad. Pompey had been forced to fill this moat
to bring on his battering rams. His assault lasted for three
months. According to Josephus, Herod had replaced the old
fort by a 'massive castle' built on a 'huge base'. Josephus describes the Antonia as dominating the Temple as the Temple
dominated the city.

Beneath the Antonia's north-western tower lay two huge cisterns, the Twin Pools. (Their name, we may recall, confused
Josephus's Greek translators, who believed he meant they were
shaped like a bird.) The western pool measured 165 by 20 feet,
and the eastern 127 by 20 feet. Above these pools lay two
courts paved with heavy stones. The Twin Pools and the paved
courts remain intact. The western court has been identified as
the Lithostrotos, Pilate's Place of Judgment.

On my visit to Jerusalem I inspected both the Pools and the
Courts. They lie beneath the Convent of the Sisters of Zion,
which occupies part of the site of the Antonia. I also examined
the southern part of its site, which can be seen from within
the precincts of the Muslim Mosque. I noticed the outcrop of
rock which once formed the base of the fortress.

The cisterns beneath the fortress were fed by a conduit
running from the north. They are of special interest. From one
of them John of Gischala tunnelled, as Josephus describes:

But while the engines were being brought up, John from
within had undermined the ground from Antonia right up
to the earthworks, supporting the tunnels with props, and
thus leaving the Roman works suspended; having then
introduced timber besmeared with pitch and bitumen he
set the whole mass alight. The props being consumed, the
mine collapsed in a heap, and with a tremendous crash
the earthworks fell in. At first dense volumes of smoke

arose with clouds of dust, the fire being smothered by the debris, but as the materials which crushed it were eaten away, a vivid flame now burst forth. The Romans were in consternation at this sudden catastrophe and dispirited by the enemy's ingenuity. Moreover, coming at the moment when they imagined victory within their grasp, the casualty damped their hopes of ultimate success. It seemed useless to fight the flames, when even if they were extinguished their earthworks were overwhelmed.

John had halted the assault on the Antonia. Simon, at his part of the defence line, was equally vigilant. The Tenth and Fifteenth Legions had propelled their siege towers up the earthworks. They were battering the wall. Simon launched a counterattack. Three brave men snatched up torches and rushed forth against these engines. They neither turned aside nor slackened their charge. They plunged into the Roman ranks and set fire to the siege towers; 'assailed by shots and sword-thrusts from every quarter, nothing could move them from the field of danger until the fire had caught hold of the machines'. The towering flames and the roar of the conflagration brought the Romans hurrying from their encampments.

Disregarding their own safety, the Jews fought to prevent the rescuers from extinguishing the flames: 'on the one side were the Romans striving to drag the battering engines out of the fire, their wicker shelters all ablaze; on the other, the Jews holding on to them despite the flames, clutching the red-hot iron and refusing to relinquish the rams'.

Unable to save their engines and themselves enveloped in flames, the Romans retreated. The Jews hotly pursued them. Joined by fresh bands and flushed with success, they pressed on with uncontrolled impetuosity. They reached the Roman entrenchments, grappling with the sentries. These, Josephus explains, 'are stationed in front of every camp and come under a severe Roman law that he who quits his post under any pretext whatsoever dies'. The sentries stood firm, preferring heroic death to ignominious execution. Their resolute bearing halted the flight of their comrades. The fugitives dragged up the artillery, keeping at bay the masses of Jews who came surging up the slopes. They grappled with the Romans and flung themselves bodily against the ramparts. But their rash daring was no match against Roman discipline. Titus attacked them in the flank. The Jews resolutely withstood the new threat, both contenders becoming engulfed in the dust raised by their conflict and soon unable to distinguish friend from foe. In the excess of their fury, says Josephus, the Romans might have succeeded in wiping out the entire Jewish host had they not, anticipating the turn of the battle, retreated into the city.

The Romans were deeply dejected. Their earthworks had been demolished, their siege towers set on fire. In one hour they had lost the fruits of their long labour; 'many despaired of ever carrying the town by assault'. Titus called a council of war. Some officers advised that he should bring up his entire army and try to carry the walls by storm. They argued that the Jews would be powerless to resist a mass attack. The cautious officers advised recourse to a blockade, to starve out the defenders. They claim that there was no contending with desperate men who prayed to die by the sword in preference to the 'harsher fate in store' if they were vanquished.

Titus hesitated. To remain totally inactive with so large an army seemed undignified. To storm the walls seemed unnecessary. Left alone, the Jews would destroy themselves. He reviewed the situation; lack of materials made it difficult to build further earthworks and it would also be difficult to guard against sallies. He could encompass the whole city with his troops. But the extent and nature of the ground would expose one section or another of his army to the risk of sudden attack. The Jews by their greater knowledge of the terrain might contrive secret exits. (That such subterranean methods of egress existed is indicated by the escape of several Zealots following the fall of the city.) Titus feared, states Josephus, that the story of his success would be diminished by delay, and rapidity was essential for renown.

Titus decided on a compromise. If the Romans wished to combine speed and security they must encompass the city with a siege wall. Only so could every exit be blocked. Wasted by famine, the Jews would then fall easy prey. The Romans chose the mammoth task of encompassing Jerusalem by building a siege wall. Their decision was a tremendous tribute to the tenacity and valour of its defenders.

Titus ordered the legions to build the wall. They vied with one another to complete their respective portions, turning the task into a game in which Titus acted as umpire. Josephus describes the course of the wall of circumvallation. Starting from the Camp of the Assyrians it ran across the lower part of the New City. It continued through the recently captured Second Wall, across the Kidron Valley and up the Mount of Olives. Then, bending south, it ran along the slopes of the opposing hills. From there it inclined westwards, sweeping round the city, enclosing the western and northern ramparts of the First Wall. The wall was thirty-nine furlongs (about five miles) in length. It included thirteen forts, whose united circumference amounted to ten furlongs (or just over one mile). It must have enclosed the city as tightly as possible, taking into consideration the undulations of the ground. It was completed in three days. The rapidity of its construction, Josephus says, was 'well-nigh incredible'. It became a legendary feat.

Titus made a tour of inspection each evening to see that the wall was fully guarded and patrolled. Its strangling effect was quickly felt by the city. Already Jerusalem was a city of death and silence. Every egress was cut off. The famine increased. Parents and children roamed the streets like phantoms. The roofs were thronged with women and babies exhausted by hunger. The alleys filled with the corpses of the aged, the ravines were choked with dead. Relieved of the fear of sudden attack and themselves plentifully supplied with food, the Romans were in high spirits. They again displayed their superabundance to the eyes of the famished citizens who thronged the walls.

Still the Jews refused to unite. John of Gischala overcame Eleazar. Now Simon turned on the citizens of the peace party who had invited him into the city. He seized Mattathias, 'one of the chief priests', probably that Mattathias who had been High Priest in A.D. 62. Following the murder of Ananus, Mattathias had won the esteem and confidence of the people. Simon accused him of secretly siding with the Romans and condemned him to death along with his three sons. He refused the victim's request—as a favour because Mattathias had opened the gates for Simon—to be slain first. His sons were slaughtered before his eyes. Mattathias was then led to the wall to see, Simon remarked, whether his Roman friends would assist him. Then he was killed. Josephus considers it a remarkable concession that he was not tortured.

One of Simon's lieutenants, a man named Jude, posed a serious threat. Horrified by the murder of Mattathias, he suggested to comrades with whom he held a tower that they surrender to the Romans. He solicited their co-operation with the remarkable argument that Simon could suffer no great harm 'if he is brought the sooner to justice'. Learning of his plot, Simon forestalled Jude. He slew him in full view of the Romans.

Another incident involved Josephus. He went to the wall to persuade the Jews to surrender. He was struck on the head by a stone and fell insensible to the ground, to the delight of the rebels. They believed they had killed the man 'for whose blood they thirsted most' and rushed out to seize the body. Titus hurried to the rescue of his friend. The rumour that Josephus was dead spread through the city. It dejected those, he says, whom he had given courage to desert. It reached his imprisoned mother. Fearing her guards, she said, 'I had no joy of him in his lifetime.' But privately she lamented his death because she had been denied his burial. Josephus recovered from the blow and returned to the wall, where the sight of the 'fully recovered Josephus' thrilled the citizens and filled the rebels with dismay.

The Romans, whom Josephus has previously described as jubilant and confident, again became dispirited—perhaps because Titus was anxious to spare the Jerusalem survivors and wished to slow the pace of the city's capture. Shortly, however, he renewed the assault. He began to raise four much larger embankments against the Antonia. (Apparently he had now abandoned his pressure on the First Wall in order to concentrate the whole effort against the key fortress.) But his soldiers were hampered in this enterprise by dearth of materials since all the trees within a radius of twelve miles had already been cut down.

Lacking wooden reinforcements, some of the earthworks collapsed. Again the Romans feared they would never take the city.

John of Gischala now sent out a band to attack the siege towers which the Romans were preparing to push up the embankment they had raised against the Antonia's north-western tower. The sally ended in failure. This may have been due to improved Roman tactics. They drew themselves up in stout array, completely screening the siege engines with their bodies, leaving no loopholes through which the Jews could insert their firebrands. Their accurate artillery fire damped the ardour of of the Jews, who fled rather than come to close quarters with the serried Roman ranks. Reviling each other as cowards, the Jews retired within the fortress.

This skirmish took place on July 20. That day the Romans launched their final assault on the Antonia. Josephus supplies an inadequate account of the battle, failing to explain the course of the operations—how the Romans overcame the defences and took three of the towers.

The Romans brought up their siege towers under a hail of stones and missiles. The fortress, however, resisted the battering. The Romans tried another method. They formed a *testudo*, the device by which a number of soldiers protected their backs by interlocking their shields. Under its cover the contingent crept to a tower wall. Wielding crowbars, they succeeded in dislodging four stones at its base. Night suspended their labours. During the hours of darkness the tower, its foundations weakened, collapsed into the tunnel which John had previously mined. Daybreak disclosed another wall which the Jews had built within the first. The Romans feared to assault it—for 'manifestly destruction awaited its first assailants'.

Titus exhorted his soldiers to daring. Once the Antonia was captured the city would be won. Still his troops held back, except for one man, a Syrian named Sabinus. He showed himself 'mighty of hand, and in spirit the bravest of men'. 'Yet,' thought Josephus, 'anyone seeing him before that day and judging him from his outward appearance would not have taken him even for a soldier. His skin was black, his flesh shrunk and emaciated; but within that slender frame, far too straight for its native prowess, there dwelt an heroic soul.'

Stepping from the ranks, Sabinus offered to scale the new wall. Only eleven others joined him. Extending his shield above his head and drawing his sword, Sabinus climbed the rubble ahead. The Jews threw down javelins and arrows and huge stones, sweeping away some of Sabinus's dauntless men. Beneath the hail of darts, Sabinus did not slacken his pace until he had gained the summit of the wall. The Jews fled, dumbfounded by his strength and intrepidity and imagining that more men came behind him.

Sabinus now stood on top of the wall which so far he alone had climbed. Then he slipped and fell headlong, striking the ground on the other side with a tremendous crash. The noise halted the Jews. Seeing Sabinus prostrate and alone, they assailed him from all sides. He rose upon his knee, screening his body with his shield. He held off his attackers, wounding many, 'but soon under his numerous wounds his arms became paralysed and at length, buried under missiles, he gave up his life'. Stimulated by their success, the Jews returned to the wall. They threw stones which crushed three of Sabinus's comrades. The remaining eight were all wounded. The Romans carried them back to camp.

But the Jews failed to hold the vital wall. Two days later, in the dead of the night, twenty legionaries together with the standard-bearer of the Fifth Legion, two troopers, and a trumpeter, crept noiselessly over the ruins of the tower. They cut down the sleeping Jewish sentries, scaling the wall. They ordered the trumpeter to sound. 'Thereupon the other guards suddenly started to their feet and fled, before any had noted what number had ascended, for the panic and the trumpet call led them to imagine that the enemy had mounted in force.' Titus heard the trumpet. He called his troops to arms and, followed by his officers and a number of picked men, climbed to the top of the wall.

Thus Josephus dismissed the vital action of the siege. From his imprecise account we may conclude that, despairing of victory, the Jews abandoned the Antonia fortress almost without a fight. Probably the strength of the siege towers was too great for the defenders to overcome. The Romans, in any case, had battered the fortress into a useless ruin.

The Romans had won the Antonia. The Jews fled to the Temple through the 'mine' excavated by John. Josephus probably meant that they used the secret passages constructed by Herod the Great to link the fortress to the Temple.

Eighteen

The Temple-
Storm Centre
of the Siege

The crisis forced the Jews to combine. Pouring through the Antonia, the Romans came face to face with both factions. Simon Gioras had brought his troops to join John of Gischala in the Temple. They stood drawn up in separate divisions. They sought to stem the Roman advance by prodigious strength and spirit. Josephus says, 'they held that the entry of the Romans into the Sanctuary meant final capture, while the latter regarded it as the prelude to victory'.

So the armies clashed in desperate struggle round the entrances, the Romans pressing on to take possession also of the Temple, the Jews thrusting them back upon the Antonia. Missiles and spears were useless to both belligerents. Drawing their swords, they closed with each other, and in the mêlée it was impossible to tell on which side either party was fighting, the men being all jumbled together and intermingled in the confined area, and their shouts, owing to the terrific din, falling confusedly on the ear. There was great slaughter on either side, and the bodies and armour of the fallen were trampled down and crushed by the combatants. And always, in whichever direction rolled the veering tide of war, were heard the cheers of the victors and the wailings of the routed. Room for flight or pursuit there was none; dubious turns on the scale and shifting of position were the sole incidents in this confused contest. Those in front had either to kill or be killed, there being no retreat, for those in the rear in either army pressed their comrades forward, leaving no intervening space between the combatants. At length, Jewish fury prevailing over Roman skill, the whole line began to waver. For they had been fighting from the ninth hour of the night until the seventh of the day; the Jews in full strength, with the peril of capture as an incentive to gallantry, the Romans with but a portion of their forces, the legions upon whom the present combatants were dependent having not yet come up. It was therefore considered sufficient for the present to hold the Antonia.

Reluctant as usual to explain the action, Josephus kept his eyes open for the heroic detail. The Bithynian Centurion Julianus, seeing the Romans waver, leaped from the wall of the Antonia. Single-handed he drove back the Jews. He forced them across the Temple forecourt. To the Jews such strength and courage appeared super-human. They fled before Julianus, who came charging through their scattered ranks, slaying all he overtook. But fate overtook him too. His nailed shoes slipped on the paved court. He fell on his back, his armour clashing as he struck the stones. The noise brought the fugitives to a halt. The Romans watching on the Antonia stood spellbound. The Jews crowded around the hero, striking him with their spears and swords. Julianus parried some blows, stabbing with his sword the assailants who thrust him down. But the helmet and cuirass protecting his body merely prolonged his death agony. At length he succumbed, alone and unaided, his body and limbs hacked and torn. His courage was matched by two of John's men, and five of Simon's. Josephus names the heroes as James, commander of the Idumaeans, and two Zealots, Simon and Jude, both sons of Ari.

Following the death of Julianus, the Jews routed the Romans. They retreated within the Antonia, and Titus ordered its foundations to be destroyed to provide his army with easy access to the Temple.

The Temple now became the storm centre of the siege. It was built, says Tacitus, like a citadel. It had well-constructed walls of its own and even the colonnades around the inner Sanctuary provided splendid defence.

Josephus, virtually our only source of information about this famous shrine, becomes reasonably lucid in his description of the Temple, with only occasional lapses into his habitual ambiguity and exaggeration. Another account, in the *Mishnah* tractate *Middoth*, was written three hundred years after the Temple's destruction but supplies some further details. Josephus tends to dwell on the architectural beauties of the building to the exclusion of its strength as a fortress.

Built by King Solomon about 959 B.C., the Temple remained intact until 586 B.C., when it was destroyed by King Nebuchadnezzar's Babylonians in their capture and sack of Jerusalem. On returning from Babylonian captivity fifty years later, the Jews built a new edifice known as Zerubbabel's Temple. Little is known about this structure except that it probably followed the earlier plan. The building was twice plundered and profaned. In 167 B.C. the Seleucid king, Antiochus Epiphanes, committed 'the abomination of desolation' by erecting a pagan altar. In 63 B.C. the Roman general Pompey, after a siege of three months, entered the Holy of Holies. He touched nothing, out of respect for the Jewish religion. But a pagan had set his unclean feet in God's Sanctuary.

Herod the Great rebuilt the Temple, both to please his subjects and to create a building of unusual beauty by which he might be remembered. The work begun in 20–19 B.C. was not fully completed until A.D. 64. Herod doubled the size of the original platform and extended its thick walls. He embanked slopes of the hill to enclose a trapezoid-shaped area measuring 523 yards on the west, and 327 yards on the north. Of Herod's sustaining walls, twenty-five courses still rise above ground. Today they are being excavated down to bedrock on the southern slopes of the hill, where the Herodian style of building is recognizable by the size and thickness of the stone blocks, some of which measure thirty to thirty-five feet. In 1969 I descended into the trenches which expose the original foundations. This great wall enclosed the southern, eastern, and western sides of the Temple, and two-thirds of the northern side, to the Antonia fortress at its north-western corner.

The southern wall contained two gates. From the western wall two viaducts spanned the Central Valley, their arches still visible in the 'Wailing Wall', where pious Jews mourn even today the destruction of the Temple by Titus. The eastern wall, facing the Mount of Olives, contained the Golden Gate, the northern wall one gate. According to Josephus it was never used.

These massive walls rose 20 feet above the Temple platform. They were flanked by porticos: roofed galleries supported by two rows of pillars. Each pillar was 50 feet thick and 40 feet high. The area within the walls and surrounding the Sanctuary was named the Court of the Gentiles. To it non-Jews were admitted but forbidden, under penalty of death, to progress further. Women were restricted to the 'Outer Court'. This was the first of several enclosed spaces which, as the worshipper progressed, became holier and holier. The Women's Court was surrounded by a balustrade containing four gates, one each on the north and south and two on the east. One of those on the east was called the Beautiful Gate because it was made of brass. It was the largest, being 80 feet high and 70 feet wide. Through this gate male Jews entered the Court of Israel. At its centre rose a flight of fifteen circular steps leading to the Court of the Priests. There stood the Altar of Burnt Sacrifice, which covered the sacred rock, the site of the threshing floor purchased by King David from Araunah the Jebusite. Twelve more steps, surmounted by an arch 150 feet high and wide, led to the Holy Place. This was guarded by a great door plated with gold. There stood the Altar of Incense, the Table of Shewbread, and the Seven Branched Candlestick—the cherished utensils of the Temple ritual. From the Holy Place the High Priest, and he alone on the Day of Atonement, entered the Holy of Holies, God's abode. The flat roof spiked with golden pinnacles (to discourage pollution by birds) rose to the height of 150 feet. The main Temple was surrounded by thirty-eight small chambers. The whole building, says Josephus, looked like 'a mountain covered with snow', so dazzling was its white marble. It symbolized the invincible power of Yahweh, the Jewish God.

The Temple also represented the city's ultimate defence. God, the Jews believed, would not permit His Sanctuary to fall into impious hands. Yet terrible were the portents of evil. Josephus says that the people were deluded by numerous false prophets, charlatans, and pretended messengers of the Deity. As a result they disregarded the plain warnings of God. For more than a year, too, a comet resembling a sword had hung over Jerusalem. For half an hour one night the Altar and Sanctuary had been illuminated by a brilliant and unearthly light. At a feast a cow had given birth to a lamb.

On another occasion the eastern gate of the Temple—the Beautiful Gate—had opened of its own accord though normally twenty men could scarcely move it. The Captain of the Temple had difficulty in shutting it again. This omen had been taken by the uninitiated to mean that God had opened the gate to receive His blessing. The learned, however, interpreted the phenomenon as a forewarning of the coming desolation of the Sanctuary.

Even before the start of hostilities, at the Feast of the Tabernacles in A.D. 62, there had appeared an even more miraculous phenomenon, one passing all belief. (He would not tell the story, says Josephus, had he not heard it from many eyewitnesses.) From before sunset chariots had been seen in the sky. Armed battalions had been observed hurtling through the clouds, encompassing cities. At the Feast of the Passover, the officiating priests had heard within the Temple first a commotion and then a din, followed by voices crying, 'We are departing.'

Even more frightening were the predictions of two ancient oracles. One foretold that, when the Romans had reduced the Temple to a square, the city and the Sanctuary would be taken. The demolition of the Antonia had reduced the area of the Temple to a square, he points out. Worse still, the Jews had been deluded, says Josephus, by the ambiguous oracle in their scriptures (which, he fails to say) foretelling that a man from Judaea would become ruler of the world. The Jews had interpreted it to mean a man of their own race. But the prophecy had been fulfilled by the proclamation on Jewish soil of Vespasian as Emperor.

More profoundly significant was the cessation of all sacrifice, a rite performed in the Jerusalem Temple for hundreds of years. Early in August, says Josephus, no priest remained to undertake the ritual slaughter. But three weeks later he records the presence of many priests in the Temple. Scarcity of animals rather than lack of priests may have been the true explanation. The famine may have overcome even Jewish reverence for the sanctity of established custom.

Titus sent Josephus to talk with John of Gischala, offering the same terms as before and telling John 'that if he was obsessed with a criminal passion for battle, he was at liberty to come out with as many men as he chose and fight, without involving the city and the Sanctuary in his own ruin'. John replied that he did not fear capture, since the city was God's. Josephus's exhortations—his words were broken by sobs—moved many of the better citizens. Some succeeded in escaping from the doomed city. They included two ex-High Priests and other notable men. (It is remarkable that these prominent citizens had survived the reign of terror—which may, then, not have been as terrible as Josephus makes out.) Titus sent these refugees to the town of Gophna, twelve miles north of Jerusalem. John claimed they had been slaughtered and Titus was forced to bring them back and parade them before the walls to deny John's slander. The sight of these refugees incited many others to leave the city. Despairing of the insurgents' surrender, Titus determined to resume hostilities.

Josephus's narrative again requires interpretation. Though the Romans had captured the Antonia, its ruins presented an obstacle to the advance of the legions, and its demolition occupied seven days. While waiting for a road to be engineered, Titus attempted a night attack. He commanded the Tribune Sextus Vettulenus to penetrate the forecourt of the Temple, between the fortress and the Sanctuary, hoping to find the Jews asleep and off their guard.

But the Jewish guards were awake and vigilant. They alerted their comrades, who dashed out, engaging the Romans in a fierce and confused struggle in which both sides were unable to distinguish friend from foe. Interlocking their shields, the legionaries then charged by companies. The Jews fell back, each man in the darkness mistaking every returning comrade for an advancing Roman. Sunrise revealed the true situation. Forming a line, the Jews stopped the Roman advance. The contest deteriorated into a static fight. There was no room for manoeuvre, so cramped was the space—like a battle on a stage, thought Josephus, watching from the height of the Antonia. In time the action was broken off by mutual consent. Josephus again paid tribute to Jewish bravery, singling out several heroes: two of Simon's men, two Idumaeans, two of John's contingent and 'of the Zealots, Simon the son of Ari'.

Beyond the information that the foundations of the Antonia had been knocked down and a broad ascent made to the Temple, Josephus leaves us in doubt as to the exact situation. His muddled account of the ensuing action is no more enlightening.

The Romans, it seems, attempted simultaneously to assault the Sanctuary and surmount the porticos which surrounded the Temple platform. Approaching what Josephus calls the 'first wall', by which he probably meant the outer wall of the Sanctuary, the legions started to raise embankments. One faced the 'north-west angle of the Inner Temple'. Another stood over against the 'northern hall which stood opposite the two gates'. The third was built opposite the western portico of the outer court, and the fourth opposite the northern portico. This work progressed slowly, it being necessary to convey timber from a distance of twelve miles.

The Romans again suffered from Jewish stratagems. One band of Jews sallied out from the city, cutting off a party of Roman horsemen who had turned their horses loose to graze. The Jews succeeded in carrying off several animals. Titus executed one of the cavalrymen as a warning of the need for greater vigilance. Another Jewish contingent climbed the Mount of Olives, hoping to catch the Roman sentries off guard. After a sharp contest they were driven back down the ravine. A solitary trooper urging his horse at great speed seized and took captive a Jewish youth. He took his prize to Titus, who ordered the boy's execution.

The Jews set fire to the north-western porticos of the Temple —those which connected it to the Antonia. They hacked down another part, with the intention of denying its use to the Romans. They set alight the adjoining porticos. The conflict raged incessantly. Small parties from both sides sallied out to attack one another. Rather than explain what was taking place,

Josephus tells yet another anecdote.

One of Simon's men, Jonathan, 'a man of mean stature and despicable appearance, undistinguished by birth or otherwise', emerged from a gate on the western wall to challenge the best of the Romans in single combat. The majority of the Romans were loath to engage a man who courted death. His defeat would represent no great exploit and his victory would bring ignominy, even death, to an opponent. A trooper named Pudens nonetheless leaped forward to engage the audacious Jew. Jonathan quickly despatched him, trampling upon the body and jeering at the Romans. His ridicule incensed the Centurion Priscus. Bending his bow he transfixed Jonathan with an arrow.

Heroic deeds, ruses, and stratagems fascinated Josephus. He loved display of cunning, especially by his own people. The hiatus in the siege operations provided him with several incidents. The first occurred on August 15. Pretending to be utterly exhausted, the Jews retired from the western portico, but not before they had filled the space between the rafters and ceiling with bitumen and pitch. A number of legionaries climbed onto the vacant portico. The Jews waited until its roof was packed with men, then set fire to it below. The leaping flames caught the imprudent soldiers helpless as their comrades watched in consternation. Some of the victims of the Jewish ruse threw themselves into the city. Others jumped into the Temple forecourt, landing in the midst of the exulting Jews. Yet others remained where they were, preferring to perish from fire or by their own swords. For these doomed men, says Josephus, the only consolation was the grief of their comrades. 'And every man carrying with him like some splendid obsequies these cries and the emotion of Titus, thus cheerfully expired.'

The last rooftop survivor was a youth named Longinus. He shed lustre on the whole tragedy by proving himself the bravest of all. Admiring his prowess, the Jews invited him to jump down, pledging him his life. But from the Antonia fortress his brother Cornelius implored him not to disgrace his reputation or Roman arms. Longinus slew himself. Another soldier, Artonius, saved himself by an artifice. He called at the top of his voice to his friend Lucius, 'I leave you heir to all my property if you come and catch me.' When Lucius ran up, Antonius plunged from his height, striking and killing his friend.

This disaster had a beneficial result for the Romans in making them less responsive to Jewish stratagem. The flames had consumed nearly all the western portico. The Jews hacked down the remaining section. Next day the Romans burned the whole of the northern portico right up to the eastern wall which overlooked the Kidron ravine. The object of these manoeuvres is hard to discern. Presumably the Romans destroyed the porticos to deny their use to the Jews.

By August 27 the Romans were ready to assail the Sanctuary. For six days the 'most redoubtable of all the siege engines' had been incessantly battering the wall without effect, so massive were its stones. More rams were brought against the western wall. A party of Romans set out to undermine the foundations of the northern gate. By great exertion they succeeded in extricating a few stones, but the gate itself held firm. Despairing of these tactics, the Romans brought up scaling ladders, mounting the porticos that surrounded the building. The Jews waited until the Romans showed themselves, then vigorously attacked them, slaying those who had climbed up, hurling others headlong. They tilted the ladders, dashing the climbers to the ground. The Jews themselves suffered considerable casualties. Eventually the Romans retired. Both armies had fought gallantly, states Josephus. He singled out for special praise Simon Gioras's nephew, one of the many Eleazars, whose name he thus recorded for posterity.

Two of Simon's most bloodthirsty lieutenants seized the opportunity to desert. They hoped for pardon because they were abandoning their comrades at the moment of success. Though he perceived their knavish trick, Titus kept his promise to spare deserters. But he put these men on a different footing from others who had previously abandoned the Jewish cause.

The Sanctuary was too strong to storm, Titus believed. He ordered its gates to be fired. The flames melted the silver with which the great door was embellished. It caught the woodwork and spread to the surrounding porticos. The encircling fire dismayed and paralysed the Jews, who did nothing to extinguish it. Next day, Titus ordered the fire to be put out. It had destroyed the intervening porticos, allowing his army to make a road through the shattered gate. Titus called his officers into council.

Titus and his generals, the commanders of the legions, the chief of staff Tiberius Alexander, and the Procurator of Judaea Marcus Antonius Julianus, debated the fate of the Temple. There are two very different versions of this conference. One is supplied by Josephus. Another is found in the *Chronicle* of the fifth-century Christian historian Sulpicius Severus. It is usually attributed to Tacitus, from whose lost book Sulpicius Severus may have derived it. Or Severus may have drawn, as Tacitus probably did, upon the writing of Marcus Antonius. He wrote about the Jews, and his books were still extant in A.D. 240. Severus would not have dared to contradict Josephus unless he had drawn upon an impeccable authority.

Josephus shows Titus as wishing to spare the Temple and angered by its accidental destruction. The sycophant may have published a false report in order to praise his patron's clemency. Josephus did not attend the conference and he may have unintentionally misinterpreted the report he received.

If Josephus can be believed, some officers expressed the opinion that the law of war should be enforced and the Temple destroyed. The Jews, they said, would never cease rebelling while the Temple remained the focus of their beliefs. Other officers thought that if the Jews abandoned the Temple it should be saved. If it were to be used as a fortress, however, it should be burned. Titus declared that even if the Jews fought from it he would not wreak vengeance on an inanimate object—not under any circumstances would he destroy so magnificent a building. Its loss would deny the Romans an ornament to their Empire. Persuaded by this argument, says Josephus, Tiberius Alexander and two of the generals came over to that view.

Sulpicius Severus provides another and possibly a more reasonable explanation:

It is said that Titus first called a council and deliberated whether he should destroy such a mighty temple. For some thought that a consecrated shrine which was famous beyond all other works of men, ought not to be razed, arguing that its preservation would bear witness to the moderation of Rome, while its destruction would forever brand her cruelty. Yet others, including Titus himself, opposed, holding the destruction of this temple to be a prime necessity in order to wipe out more completely the religion of the Jews and the Christians; for they urged that these religions, although hostile to each other, nevertheless sprang from the same sources; the Christians had grown out of the Jews: if the root were destroyed, the stock would easily perish.

Severus's statement that the two religions were reciprocally hostile represents opinion current at the time he wrote.

If Severus records the correct version of Titus's intent, it indicates that the Romans considered the Christians were as responsible as their fellow Jews for the instigation of the revolt. Christian as well as Jewish politico-religious fanaticism would be curbed by the destruction of the Sanctuary. If this is the true explanation, it adds significantly to our knowledge of the participation of the Jewish Christians in their nation's revolt. The followers of Jesus differed from their fellow Jews only in their peculiar belief that their dead Messiah would return to complete his mission. That was to restore the kingdom to Israel, exactly the enterprise which the Zealots and the other politico-religious sects were determined to achieve.

Titus ordered his soldiers to storm the ruined gate. Their advance imperilled the Sanctuary. The Jews sallied from the eastern gate, charging the Romans' left flank. The Romans closed their ranks, forming a shield wall. Though pressed back by the number and fury of their assailants, they stubbornly resisted the Jewish attack. Titus then withdrew his soldiers in preparation for the final assault. When Titus left the scene to return to camp, the fight began again. The Jews sallied out once more; the Romans threw them back, pressing them against the walls of the Sanctuary. Josephus tells the story:

At this moment, one of the soldiers, awaiting no orders and with no horror of so dread a deed, but moved by some supernatural impulse, snatched a brand from the burning timber and, hoisted up by one of his comrades, flung the fiery missile through a low golden door which gave access on the north side to the chambers surrounding the Sanctuary. As the flames shot up, a cry, as poignant as the tragedy, arose from the Jews who flocked to the rescue, lost to all thought of self-preservation, all husbanding of strength, now that the object of all their past vigilance was vanishing.

Titus was resting in his tent when the news reached him. Starting up, he ran to the Temple followed by his generals, determined, says Josephus, to stop the conflagration. Reaching the burning building, he shouted and gesticulated to his soldiers to extinguish the fire. They neither heeded his shouts, drowned in the din, nor noticed his beckoning hand, distracted as they were by the fire and their own fury.

Crushed together about the entrances, many were trampled down by their companions; many, stumbling on the still hot and smouldering ruins of the porticos, suffered the fate of the vanquished. As they drew nearer to the Sanctuary they pretended not even to hear Caesar's orders and shouted to those in front of them to throw in their firebrands. The insurgents, for their part, were now powerless to help; and on all sides was carnage and flight. Most of the slain were civilians, weak and unarmed people, easily butchered where they were caught. Around the altar a pile of corpses was accumulating; down the steps of the Sanctuary flowed a stream of blood, and the bodies of the victims killed above went sliding to the bottom.

Unable to restrain his frenzied soldiers, Titus rushed into the Sanctuary. He penetrated into the Holy Place, where the flames had not yet reached. He urged the soldiers to quench the flames which were now consuming the surrounding chambers. But nothing, not even the clubs wielded by his escort, availed; the men's respect for their general was overcome by their hatred for the Jews and their lust for battle. The end was precipitated by one soldier. He thrust a firebrand into the hinges of a gate leading into the Holy Place. At once a flame shot up. The Sanctuary was doomed.

The fire spread through the building, leaping high in the air. Its roar was heard throughout the city. To the horrified spectators it seemed that the whole Temple hill was boiling over from its base, one mass of flame. The war cries of the soldiers sweeping forward, the howls of the rebels encircled by fire and sword, the shrieks of the wounded, and the groans of the dying rose above the general clamour. From the Jews massed on the western hill arose a wail of terror. Scanning the skies they awaited the saving miracle.

Dr R. H. Charles (in *The Revelation of St John*) suggests that the eleventh chapter of the Apocalypse preserves a fragment of Zealot prophecy. If so, they believed that, while the outer courts of the Temple might be trodden underfoot by Gentiles, Yahweh would not suffer His Sanctuary to be touched by impious heathen feet. The Zealots expected the saving miracle, as must have the Christians. But God did not answer. The crucified Messiah did not reappear at the head of legions of angels. The Zealots, the Christians, and the other revolutionaries had pinned their faith on a false hope. The fall of the Temple was a fatal blow to the logic of their belief. Streaming far and wide, the roar of the flames echoed from the surrounding hills, the funeral pyre of blighted hopes.

More awful than the uproar were the sufferings. While the Temple blazed, the victors plundered and slew. They showed no pity for age or reverence for rank; children, greybeards, soldiers, priests, all were massacred. The stream of blood, states the eyewitness, was greater than the flames, the slain more numerous than the slayers. To pursue the fugitives, the soldiers had to climb over heaps of corpses.

The Temple's defenders—John's Galileans, Eleazar's Zealots, and Simon's Idumaeans—pushed past the Romans, forcing their way through the crowd of fugitives, escaping by the viaducts into the city. The priests stripped the spikes from the Sanctuary, hurling them at the Romans. Survivors huddled on the porticos, plunged into the fire, or remained on the wall until they were engulfed. A boy called to the Roman soldiers, begging for water. Taking pity on this youth, they promised him protection, offering him a vessel. He seized it and raced back to his comrades, the soldiers cursing his perfidy. He had broached no covenant, he shouted. The soldiers marvelled to see so much cunning in one so young. The last surviving priests came down, imploring Titus to spare their lives. He refused. The time for pardon had gone and it behooved priests to perish with their Temple.

The Romans saw it was useless to fight the flames. They set fire to the remainder of the buildings, the porticos, the outer gates, and finally the Treasury, repository of Jewish wealth. Still part of the outer portico remained intact. On it clustered a host (six thousand, says Josephus) of refugees, mostly women and children and a smaller group of men. The enraged soldiers set fire to it; not a soul escaped. Josephus was informed that that very day a false prophet had told these wretched people that God had commanded them to go to the Temple to receive there His tokens of deliverance.

Making a quick and approximate calculation, Josephus estimated that the Temple, built first by King Solomon, had survived for 1,130 years, 7 months, and 15 days. It perished finally on August 30, anniversary of its earlier burning by the soldiers of Nebuchadnezzar, King of Babylon. From A.D. 70 the Jews have mourned their loss on the 9th day of the Hebrew month Ab.

The legions set up their standards in the Temple courts opposite the eastern gate and sacrificed to them, acclaiming Titus as *imperator*—Emperor. Once again the Abomination of Desolation stood where it ought not. So glutted were the soldiers with plunder, says Josephus, that throughout Syria the value of gold became depreciated by half.

From John and Simon came a message to the Roman camp, asking for a parley.

Nineteen

The Palace Bastions

Titus clambered onto the western wall of the Temple platform, overlooking the viaduct. At its western end stood John and Simon. The Jews clustered around their leaders, excited by hopes of pardon. The Roman soldiers ranged themselves beside Titus, eagerly awaiting the rebels' offer. Titus charged his troops to keep a check on their temper and to hold their fire. With an interpreter at his side, he opened the proceedings. You are justly doomed to perish, he told the two 'tyrants', as Josephus calls John and Simon. The Jews had begun the war. They had lost their country and their Sanctuary and were doomed to perish. 'Throw down your arms and surrender, and I will grant your lives,' Titus told them. John and Simon replied that they had sworn never to surrender. They asked permission to pass through the Roman lines with their wives and children, undertaking to retire to the desert. Their request roused Titus's indignation; men in their position should not dare to offer terms to the victors. They had no hope for pardon, he would not spare them. He advised them to fight and save themselves as best they could. He told his troops to sack and burn the city. They set fire to the Archives, the Temple markets, the Council Chamber, and the whole city region of Ophel nearby. The flames spread to the palace of the late Queen Helena and consumed the houses still packed with bodies of those who had died in the famine.

A number of deserters came to surrender; they included the sons and brothers of Isates, King of Adiabene. Titus held them as hostages for the allegiance of their country. Somehow, the rebels captured two Roman soldiers. One they killed and dragged through the city. The other was marked for execution. Though bound and blindfolded, he managed to escape, reaching the Roman lines. Though being taken alive was a capital crime under Roman military law, Titus could not bring himself to put the man to death. Instead he deprived him of his arms and dismissed him from his legion—a penalty severer than death to a man with any sense of shame, says Josephus.

The Romans poured from the Temple and overran the Lower Town, burning it as far down as the Pool of Siloam. But they found no loot. The rebels had carried off everything of value, proud that, with the Temple in ashes, the citizens slaughtered, and the town in flames, they had left nothing for their enemies. Josephus never flagged in entreating the rebels to spare the city and its people. The only answer he received was ridicule. Some of the rebels sought refuge in subterranean passages beneath the city. They hoped to escape after its capture.

The Romans had won the Lower City. Now they prepared to reduce the Upper, a far more formidable task. Its thickly clustered houses were dominated by the bastions of Herod's palace. Approach from the east was hindered by the Central Valley, across which Simon had built four fortress-towers during his war with John. It would be easier, thought Titus, to assault the palace from the west, from the Roman main camp. The work of raising embankments began on September 8. It was not completed until the 25th. Several incidents occurred during this interval.

Five of Simon's Idumaeans came to Titus begging his protection. Their defection, Titus thought, might force the rebel chieftain to yield. He consented to spare them, sending the Idumaeans back. Simon put all five to death. He imprisoned their leaders including their chieftain, James son of Sosas, who had brought them originally to Jerusalem. He set his men to watch the remaining Idumaeans. But his sentries were unable to check desertions and a large number escaped to the Romans. Titus spared their lives. Those who proved their citizenship were given their pardon. The rest, including women and children, were sold as slaves for a trifling sum—the market was already glutted. Titus appointed officers to screen deserters, deciding who should be sold or executed and who should be spared.

Titus's pledge of protection brought him valuable benefits. A priest, Jesus son of Thebuthi, emerged from beneath the Temple precincts with two lamp stands and various tables, bowls, and platters, all made of gold and very massive. He delivered also

the High Priest's vestments, precious stones, and the utensils of
the Temple ritual. He was followed by Phineas, the Temple
Treasurer, who handed over tunics and girdles, an abundance
of purple and scarlet material, a mass of spices, and many 'other
treasures'. These may have included the Table of Shewbread,
two silver trumpets, and the Seven Branched Candlestick. They
or their replicas were carried in the Roman Triumph in A.D. 71.

By September 25 the Romans were ready to assault Herod's
palace. It was dominated by three towers, named Hippicus,
Phasael, and Mariamne. They were placed at the spot where the
First Wall turned eastwards. Josephus claims that they were
superior in size, beauty, and strength to any in the world. The
Hippicus tower rose to the height of 120 feet. It was $37\frac{1}{2}$ feet
wide and built in square sections. Its roof contained a cistern
and was surrounded by a ring of turrets, each three feet high
and crowned with ramparts. The Phasael tower was 135 feet
high. Its solid base stands to this day. Simon had made it his
headquarters. The Mariamne tower was $82\frac{1}{2}$ feet high and 30
feet wide.

The size of these towers, states Josephus, seemed much greater
because they stood on the crest of a hill. They were of white
marble cut in blocks, each 30 feet long, 15 feet wide, and $7\frac{1}{2}$
feet deep. These were so perfectly united that each tower seemed
like a single rock 'sent up by Mother Earth and later cut and
polished by artists' hands, into shapes and angles, so invisible
from any view point was the filling of the joints'.

'No tongue could describe the magnificence of Herod's palace.'
It contained huge banqueting halls and many guest rooms.
About the interior Josephus waxed lyrical. Words could not
describe the beauty of the stones, the length of the ceiling beams,
the splendour of the ornamentation, the luxurious furnishings,
the variety of the rooms, their contents of gold and silver. On
every side were numbers of intersecting colonnades, each differ-
ing in the design of its pillars. Between them stretched green
lawns, coppices of trees, long walks, deep canals, and cisterns.
All were adorned with bronze statues gushing water, and
pigeon-cotes. Josephus found his old memories of the palace
agonizing. By the time he saw it again, it had been fired by the

rebels. No wonder the Romans believed they would never batter down these massive towers; Josephus thought they would have defied every engine of war.

The Romans did not need all their battering rams. The majority of the rebels by now despaired of holding even their near-impregnable fortress. They abandoned their ramparts and slunk away, hiding themselves in the city's subterranean tunnels. Simon and John held one tower. Its walls soon crumbled under the Romans' battering. The two chieftains, says Josephus, became paralysed by fright even before the Romans had surmounted the breach. The transformation of these men, says the hostile historian, was pitiable. Once so haughty and proud of their crimes, they were now abject and trembling. Eager to make a dash, to cut their way through the Romans, they could find no henchmen to aid them. They were impotent to fly even when told that the whole western wall had been overthrown, that the Romans had broken through and were in sight. Josephus attributes their sorry state to the power of God over unholy men. Finally, John and Simon abandoned their tower, finding refuge in the ravine below the Pool of Siloam. When they attempted to break out they were repulsed. Finally they too took refuge in the underground passages.

The victory of the Romans was now complete. They planted their standards on the captured tower and raised a shout of victory. The end had proved a much lighter task than the beginning. They could hardly believe they had overcome the massive towers without bloodshed. The soldiers rushed through the alleys massacring indiscriminately all they encountered, burning the houses or entering them in search of loot. (They found them filled with victims of the famine, and devoid of loot.) Only darkness brought an end to the killing. That night the fires spread throughout Jerusalem. By daybreak the whole city was ablaze. The conflagration did not prevent Titus from inspecting the captured city. The architectural qualities of the palace towers astonished him as they had Josephus. 'God indeed,' he told his companions, 'has been with us in this war.' Human hands and engines alone could not have conquered towers of such great breadth and vast height.

Titus ordered that only those found carrying arms and offering resistance were to be killed. The soldiers interpreted the command to include the old and the feeble. The bulk of the prisoners were paraded in the Temple forecourt. The 'seditious and the brigands' were executed. The tallest and most handsome youths were selected to grace the victor's Roman Triumph. Others over seventeen years of age were sent to labour in the mines in Egypt. A vast multitude of prisoners were despatched to various Roman provinces to be thrown to wild beasts in the theatres. The children were sold as slaves. Eleven thousand prisoners died of starvation, says Josephus, partly because of the hatred of jailers who denied them food. Others refused to eat. The total number of prisoners, states Josephus, was 97,000, and he claims that 1,100,000 people died during the siege. The majority, though of Jewish blood, were not natives of the city. To support his astronomical figures, he quotes the census taken at the Passover in the time of Cestius Gallus, when 255,600 pascal lambs had been slaughtered. By allowing an average of ten feasters for each animal, Josephus concluded that they numbered 2,700,000 people, or more correctly, 2,566,000. The besieged city, he says was packed with inhabitants. Josephus's propensity to exaggerate, as well as general improbability, makes these figures highly suspect.

The victors instituted a search for the fugitives who had concealed themselves underground. They tore up pavements and streets, slaying all they encountered. Here, too, says Josephus, were found upward of 2,000 already dead. Some had taken their own lives, others had been killed by another's hand, and yet others had died from famine. In these passages the stench was so horrible that only the most avaricious soldiers penetrated far, in search of loot. John of Gischala, the Galilean leader, was discovered dying from hunger. Now he implored that protection which he had so often spurned. It was granted—why, Josephus does not say—and John was sentenced to perpetual imprisonment. Simon Gioras delayed his fate. He and some faithful friends secured some stone-cutting tools and enough food to last for several days. They let themselves down into one of the secret passages, following the old excavation as far as it extended.

Meeting solid rock they began to dig, hoping to emerge outside the city and make their escape. But their consumption of food outpaced their tunnelling and they were forced to give up. Simon hoped to cheat the Romans by creating a scare. He dressed himself in a white tunic and rose out of the ground at the very spot whereon the Temple had formerly stood. At first the soldiers were startled by the apparition. Then they pulled themselves together, approached Simon, and asked who he was. He realized that his deception would be unmasked and asked to be taken to the general. He was led to Terentius Rufus, the new Procurator, who put him in chains and sent him to Caesarea, where Titus had gone. Titus ordered Simon to be kept for the Roman Triumph. Josephus does not mention the fate of the leader of the third faction, Eleazar son of Simon; he may have died with his Zealots in the defence of the Temple.

Before leaving Jerusalem, Titus had given orders for the city to be laid waste 'so that no one visiting the spot would believe it had once been inhabited'. Every wall and building was torn down except the three towers of Herod's Palace and a portion of the wall encircling the city on the west. These Titus retained to show posterity the strength of the defences the Romans had overcome, and to provide a fortress for the Tenth Legion, left to guard the captured city. 'Such was the end,' remarks Josephus, 'to which the frenzy of the revolutionaries brought Jerusalem,' that splendid city of world renown.

During the course of her excavations within the Old City, the British archaeologist, Dr Kathleen Kenyon, found several places filled with a jumble of stones and fallen masonry. This was the debris of the houses and walls thrown down by the Romans. In one shaft she found a hoard of coins dated between A.D. 66 and 70. They had been hidden before the city was overwhelmed, one of the few caches missed by looters. Josephus says that for several months following the siege much silver and gold was unearthed, their hiding places disclosed by prisoners.

Further evidence of the 'dramatic razing of Jerusalem' was uncovered in the ruins of a house on the slopes of the south-western hill in January 1970 (*New York Times*, January 16, 1970). Professor Nahum Avigad of the Hebrew University found two rooms which had apparently been used as a workshop. They contained two ovens, some finely carved stone jars, a set of stone weights and measuring cups, mortars and pestles, and other objects including a stone table mounted on a marble pedestal. Everywhere, Professor Avigad found evidence of intense heat—stones reddened, blackened, and yellowed from fire and a concentration of ashes. The coins precisely dated the destruction of the building. They were stamped the FIRST and SECOND years of THE REDEMPTION, A.D. 66 and 67.

On his return to Jerusalem, Titus paraded his army. He commended his soldiers for their achievement, rewarding those who had specially distinguished themselves. They had demonstrated to all mankind, he said, that 'neither the numbers of the enemy, the strength of fortresses, the magnitude of cities, nor the reckless daring and bestial savagery of antagonists' could undermine the valour of Romans. Those soldiers who had performed brilliant feats were called up by name. Titus placed crowns of gold upon their heads and presented them with gold neck-chains, little golden spears, and standards made of silver. Each was promoted to higher rank and assigned a special share of the spoils. Titus invoked blessings on the whole army. A number of oxen were sacrificed and their meat distributed to the troops. Finally, Titus distributed the legions to their future posts. The Tenth stayed in Judaea. He banished the Twelfth to take the Tenth's place on the Euphrates, as a mark of Imperial disapproval for its defeat at Beth-horon. The Fifth and Fifteenth Legions returned to Egypt.

Before sailing to Rome, Titus marched through Palestine, parading his prisoners. Some were thrown to wild beasts, others were opposed to each other in mortal combat. Despite the myriad forms of execution, says Josephus, 'all this seemed too light a penalty'.

Josephus prospered from the war. Titus had repeatedly urged him during the campaign to take whatever he wanted from the wreck of the country and granted his request for the lives of his brother and friends. Josephus found and liberated one hundred and ninety acquaintances among the prisoners assembled in the Temple forecourt. Magnanimously he took no ransom for their lives and restored their property. On a journey outside Jerusalem, Josephus recognized three friends among a group of prisoners being crucified. Titus allowed them to be taken down. Two died and one survived. This suggests that the Romans preferred the 'slow' to the 'quick' form of death by crucifixion. When a *sedile* (a seat) was provided, the victim lingered on the cross, perhaps for days. He died eventually from exposure and exhaustion. Denied the *sedile*, he succumbed quickly and in terrible agony from asphyxia. Supported by the hands alone, the weight of the body extended the chest, preventing normal breathing, and the victim writhed gasping for breath until he expired.

Josephus was also given a parcel of land in the Maritime Plain, to compensate for the loss of his possessions in the city.

Early in A.D. 71 Josephus accompanied Titus on his return to Rome. The historian was accorded great consideration by the Emperor. Vespasian gave him a lodging in the house he had formerly occupied, the privilege of Roman citizenship, a pension, and another tract of land in Judaea. His privileged position, says Josephus, excited envy and exposed him to danger. A Jew named Jonathan, who later promoted an insurrection in Cyrene, asserted on capture that he had been provided by Josephus with arms and money. Undeceived by the man's mendacity, Vespasian sentenced him to death and he was burned alive. Following Vespasian's death, Josephus continued to prosper in the reigns of his two sons, Josephus's own general Titus and Domitian. He was again accused by Jews. Domitian, the new Emperor, punished them as he did one of the historian's slaves, his son's tutor. Domitian exempted Josephus's property in Judaea from taxation, and his wife, the Empress Domitia, 'never ceased conferring favours upon me'. Josephus married three times, his second wife bearing him three children, two of whom died, and his third wife, two sons.

Josephus witnessed the Triumph of Vespasian and Titus in Rome. John and Simon, together with seven hundred other Jewish prisoners, had been brought to Italy to grace the procession. The historian found it impossible adequately to describe the multitude, variety, and magnificence of the spectacles presented to display the majesty of the Roman Empire on this occasion:

> Silver and gold and ivory in masses, wrought into all man-
> ner of forms, might be seen, not as if carried in procession,
> but flowing, so to speak, like a river; here were tapestries
> borne along, some of the rarest purple, others embroidered
> by Babylonian art with perfect portraiture; transparent
> gems, some set in golden crowns, some in other fashions,
> swept by in such profusion as to correct our erroneous sup-
> position that any of them were rare. Then, too, there were
> carried images of their gods of marvellous size and no mean
> craftsmanship, and of these not one but was of some rich
> material. Beasts of many species were led along all capari-
> soned with appropriate trappings. The numerous attendants
> conducting each group of animals were decked in garments
> of true purple dye, interwoven with gold, while those
> selected to take part in the pageant itself had about them
> choice ornaments of amazing richness. Moreover, even
> among the mob of captives, none was to be seen unadorned,
> the variety and beauty of their dresses concealing from view
> any unsightliness arising from bodily disfigurement.

Nothing in the procession, Josephus says, excited so much
astonishment as the structure of the moving stages. Many were
three or four storeys high, and the magnificence of their fabric
was a source of delight and amazement:

> For many were enveloped in tapestries interwoven with
> gold, and all had a framework of gold and wrought ivory.
> The war was shown by numerous representations, in separate
> sections, affording a very vivid picture of its episodes. Here
> was to be seen a prosperous country devastated, there whole
> battalions of the enemy slaughtered; here a party in flight,
> there others led into captivity; walls of surpassing compass
> demolished by engines, strong fortresses overpowered, cities
> with well-manned defences completely mastered and an
> army pouring within the ramparts, an area all deluged with
> blood, the hands of those incapable of resistance raised in
> supplication, temples set on fire, houses pulled down over

their owners' heads, and, after general desolation and woe, rivers flowing, not over a cultivated land, nor supplying drink to man and beast, but across a country still on every side in flames. For to such sufferings were the Jews destined when they plunged into war; and the art and magnificent workmanship of these structures now portrayed the incidents to those who had not witnessed them, as though they were happening before their eyes. On each of the stages was stationed the general of one of the captured cities in the attitude in which he was taken. A number of ships also followed.

Conspicuous among the spoils were the sacred treasures taken from the Temple, the golden Table of Shewbread, the golden Seven Branched Candlestick, various trumpets and cups, and the Scrolls of the Law. These were carried by Roman soldiers. They were followed by the captives led by John and Simon. Behind them Vespasian and Titus drove in a carriage. The Emperor's younger son, Domitian, rode on horseback.

The procession ended at the temple of Jupiter Capitolinus. It halted there, by time-honoured custom, to await the news of the execution of the enemy's general. Simon was first scourged and then strangled in the Forum. John was led away to imprisonment. The announcement that Simon was dead was greeted with universal applause. The victorious Emperor and his son offered the customary prayers. They then withdrew to their Palace on the Palatine Hill where they celebrated with a banquet.

The spoils of the Jewish Temple were deposited in the Temple of Peace, as a perpetual reminder of the might of Rome and the folly of revolt.

These sacred treasures had a chequered career. They disappeared when Rome was sacked and plundered in A.D. 455 by Genserich, King of the Vandals. Their subsequent history is legendary. One story has it that the Jews of Rome stole them from the Temple and cast them into the River Tiber, where they remain in the mud to this day. A stronger tradition relates that they were taken by Genserich to Carthage, where they remained for seventy-nine years until, on the defeat of the

Vandals, the Byzantine general Belisarius took them to Constantinople. According to yet another tradition, they were borne in triumph in A.D. 534 through Constantinople and then kept exposed for public view. But the Emperor Justinian became frightened by the warnings of the Byzantine Jews that no good could come of such sacrilege. He ordered that the sacred relics should be returned to Jerusalem. In one account they were deposited in the Greek Christian Church in that city. In another version they were lost at sea.

Some scholars claim that the treasures handed over by Jesus and Phineas were only replicas. The originals were concealed by the Zealots in A.D. 68 with the rest of the treasures.

The Emperor had demonstrated to the citizens of Rome the magnitude of the Roman victory. It was advisable to publicize the suppression of revolt throughout the Empire as well—no easy task in an age which lacked means of propaganda, but the Romans were equal to it. Minted coins circulated to every hut from the Euphrates to the British Isles. They were now engraved IVDAEA CAPTA; a palm tree symbolized Judaea. A captive Jew stood with his hands tied behind him. Upon a litter of useless shields sprawled a female prisoner, the captive daughter of Zion mourning the destruction of Jerusalem. These coins have been found throughout the lands of the ancient Roman Empire. Their circulation, however, failed to deter one band of pious pilgrims which reached Jerusalem in A.D. 71, unaware that the Temple had been destroyed.

The Romans also commemorated their great victory by the erection on the Forum of a Triumphal Arch dedicated to Vespasian and Titus. It was probably erected after the latter's death in A.D. 81, for its inscription adds 'Divine' to his name. Its two bas-reliefs depict the spoils of Jerusalem and the Emperor Vespasian in his chariot.

The Arch of Titus, as it is called, still dominates the Roman Forum, a perpetual reminder of the siege and destruction of Jerusalem by the Romans.

The Jews had fallen by the edge of the sword and been led captive into all nations. Jerusalem had been trodden down under the feet of the Gentiles.

Twenty

The Zealots'
Last Stand

Great numbers of Jews had been slain. Many had been sold into slavery. An even greater number were permitted to remain in Palestine. The Romans did not treat the general mass of survivors badly, preferring to conciliate them. They were heavily taxed and forced to do certain compulsory work, such as the upkeep of roads. The system of land tenure was changed; the Emperor sequestered the whole country, leasing the land to tenants. The leading Pharisee, Jonathan ben Zakkai, who had escaped from beleaguered Jerusalem, was permitted to keep his school at Jamnia. Talmudic references (culled by A. Buchler, *The Economic Condition of Judaea after the Destruction of the Second Temple*) indicate the survival of several notable families, some members of whom, previously rich, became very poor. The famine did not end with the siege. Folklore relates that fugitives hiding in caves fed on the bodies of the slain. Miriam, a daughter of the wealthy Nagdimon ben Gurion, was reduced to gathering barley from beneath horses' hooves. Martha, the widow of the ex-High Priest Joshua ben Gamala, was seized by soldiers. They tied her hair to the tail of a horse and forced her to run from Lydda to Jerusalem. Another legend tells the story of the son and daughter of a priest. They had been sold as slaves to different people and were reunited by chance—when they were brought together to be mated. Some Jews, as a reward for their surrender, were permitted to retain their lands. (As many as 40,000 people, Professor Buchler believes, went over to the Romans during the siege.)

Only the Zealots remained intransigent. They held out in two strongholds, at Machaerus on the eastern side of the Dead Sea and at Masada on its western bank. It is clear from Josephus's statements that both garrisons were Zealots, although as usual he is loath to employ that term. The garrison of Machaerus, he says, 'separated themselves from their alien colleagues'—the Zealot characteristic. He called the defenders of Masada *Sicarii*, his name for Zealots.

The Zealots of Masada had played no part in the revolt. Their leader, Eleazar son of Jair, considered himself the true inheritor of the Zealot ideal and may have scorned to associate himself with other groups whose beliefs he considered defective. Following the murder of Menahem at the start of the revolt, the Zealots had split into two factions. Those led by the other Eleazar had mostly died in the defence of Jerusalem. One of their number, the gallant Jude whose deeds Josephus recorded, escaped to Masada on the fall of the city. He joined Eleazar, who scorned to surrender, refusing to admit that God had deserted the Jewish cause.

It became the task of the new Legate, Lucillus Bassus, to liquidate these remaining pockets of resistance. He concentrated first on Machaerus, familiar as the site of John the Baptist's execution by Herod Antipas. Bassus led the Tenth Legion across the Jordan and around the head of the Dead Sea.

The fortress, says Josephus, was perched on a rocky eminence. Nature had contrived to render it inaccessible. It was surrounded on all sides by deep ravines, difficult to cross and utterly impossible to fill in. King Herod had encircled its crest with a wall forty feet high, and had built within a spacious palace containing beautiful apartments and many cisterns to catch and store rainwater. Its defenders believed that as long as they held the fortress they could bargain with the Romans for their lives. A casual incident led to their surrender. One of the defenders was a daring youth, yet another Eleazar who had distinguished himself in sallies, from one of which he was the last to withdraw. He loitered outside the walls, conversing with his comrades, unmindful of danger. A Roman soldier named Rufus by a sudden dash seized and carried him off, dragging him into the Roman camp. His comrades were visibly affected. They lamented and bewailed in a manner which, says Josephus, the misfortune of a mere individual seemed hardly to justify.

Bassus hoped to gain by the Jews' distress. He tried a ruse.

Eleazar was led out and preparations were made to crucify him in sight of his friends. Eleazar besought them to yield rather than leave him to undergo this most horrible of deaths. The garrison could not resist his appeal and marched out. Bassus spared them, and they departed in safety taking Eleazar with them. The citizens of the Lower Town were not included in this strange compact, however. Seeking to escape by creeping out at night, they were intercepted and cut down. Seventeen hundred were slain, and only the most courageous succeeded in getting away.

Bassus won another victory at the forest of Jardes on the west of the Dead Sea, where he cornered fugitives from Jerusalem and Machaerus. Surrounding them with his cavalry to prevent escape, Bassus sent his infantry to the wood where the Jews had taken cover. All three thousand were slain, including their general, Jude son of Ari, who had made his escape from Jerusalem 'through underground passages'.

Bassus died in A.D. 72, leaving his successor Flavius Silva to subdue Masada. Josephus does not say when Silva went there, or how long the siege lasted. It is unlikely that the Romans entered that inhospitable region until the winter rains of A.D. 73 had flooded the *wadis* and gullies. Otherwise they would have been forced to carry water from Engaddi ten miles away. It was probably from Engaddi that the Romans reached Masada, rather than by the alternative route, the one I followed from Hebron, twenty-one miles to the west.

The ground has changed little since Silva first espied the isolated, flat-topped, red limestone crag which rises 1,700 feet above the level of the Dead Sea and a mile and a half from its western shore. As the tour bus proceeded through the pitiless, parched wilderness, the rough road rising and falling and meandering through the hills, I looked ahead, anxious to glimpse the fabled 'mountain fastness'—the meaning of the name Masada. Finally, as we rounded the last bend, it burst into view ahead, slightly below the level of the road, a 'place of gaunt and majestic beauty', as Professor Yigael Yadin has described it. Behind Masada shimmered the waters of the Dead Sea. On either side rose golden-brown cliffs and dark ravines, intersected by dry watercourses. Descending the slope, the bus halted on the small plateau close to the ancient Roman headquarters camp, the outlines of which were clearly visible. From the plateau rose the embankment built by the Romans to reach the walls which still encircle the hill's summit. (This huge mound of earth reaches even now to within thirty feet of the summit. It has slipped a little during a recent earth tremor.) It is an amazing monument to Roman ingenuity and engineering skill. The modern path climbs beside the siege camp. Since the photograph in this book was taken, the Israeli army engineers have provided steps and a balustrade near the top to help visitors make the final ascent.

The earthen ramp covers the original western path to the summit. Another, the famous 'Snake Path', as Josephus named it because of its 'resemblance to that reptile in its narrowness and continual windings', zigzags up the eastern cliff. Its ascent requires one foot to be placed ahead of the other 'with destruction awaiting on every side'. Josephus may have visited Masada during his youthful sojourn in the wilderness.

Masada warrants its description as 'impregnable'. Its sheer cliffs offered no foothold to the besieger. Eleazar and his 960 Zealots must have felt secure. Surely no one could scale the cliffs and dislodge them? They were well provided with food and water. King Herod had stored provisions sufficient for 10,000 men; the dry climate had preserved this food. He had also constructed an ingenious catchment system to channel the winter floods into cisterns. Eleven of these still remain.

Herod had encircled the lozenge-shaped summit with a casement wall 4,250 feet in length. On the flat top of the hill, which extends 190 feet from north to south and 650 feet from east to west, he built store rooms, a bath-house, and a palace. He constructed an even more spectacular residence on the terraces of the northern cliff which can now be reached by balustraded steps.

A flicker of doubt may have crossed Eleazar's mind as he watched the Romans make their preparations. First they established eight camps. The outlines of these are clearly visible both on the ground and from the height of the hill. This undertaking may have occupied one week. Next day they encircled the fortress with a siege wall, 4,700 yards long. It stands now five feet high—the collapsed material, it has been calculated, would have raised it another five feet. It was intersected by five forts and by several towers. It may have taken the Tenth Legion between one and two weeks to construct. Silva had caged in the Zealots. But that was not enough.

He built an earthen ramp against the western cliff. It filled the intervening gully and reached close to the summit, as we have seen. It rose at an incline of one in three, was 300 feet long and 695 feet wide at its base. Its top was crowned with flat stones. Up this embankment the Romans pushed their 90-foot-high siege tower. Its upper tiers rose above the level of the casement wall.

Josephus does not say how long it took the Romans to build the ramp and bring up the siege tower. The Zealots, lacking artillery, could have done little to hinder its progress. From the safety of the tower, the ram battered the casement wall 'without intermission'. It made a wide breach. Behind the first wall the Zealots had built a second wall made of wooden beams laid lengthwise and in parallel rows. The intervening space was filled with earth. This made a pliable structure which ramming served only to solidify and strengthen. The soldiers on the top of the Roman tower showered down burning brands, setting the wooden wall on fire. But this method of assault nearly cost the Romans their tower. The southern wind blew the flames back against it, threatening its destruction, despite its iron casing. Then the wind suddenly veered, blowing with full force from the opposite direction and setting the wooden wall fully ablaze. Satisfied that they could storm the fortress next day, the Romans withdrew to their camp. It was May 2, A.D. 73.

Eleazar saw that all was now lost. He made a grave decision and assembled his comrades that night. He addressed them in words which Josephus learned at third hand, probably from some Roman officer. Much of it sounds like Josephus's own philosophy. But some phrases express the Zealot ideal. Reminding his comrades that they alone remained to preserve freedom, Eleazar referred to his band as 'we who have ever been instructors of the rest'. This telling phrase indicates that he considered that they alone had preserved the original Zealot teachings: 'Long since, my brave men, we determined neither to serve the Romans nor any other save God, for He alone is man's true and righteous Lord.' The time had now come to verify that resolution by action. They had the choice, he told his followers, between noble death or dishonour; his words still had not touched all his comrades' hearts—some flinched from killing wives and children and then themselves. Fired with mighty fervour, Eleazar reminded them that by death they would gain the immortality of their souls. He asked them to deny the Romans the fruits of victory.

His hearers cut their commander short. Overpowered by some uncontrollable impulse, they were in haste to do the deed. Each man was eager to outstrip his neighbour, so great was their passion to slaughter their wives, their little ones, and themselves. Nor did their ardour cool when they approached their tasks:

> For, while they caressed and embraced their wives and took their children in their arms, clinging in tears to those parting kisses, at the same instant, as though served by hands other than their own, they accomplished their purpose, having the thought of the ills they would endure under the enemy's hands to console them for their constraint in killing them. And in the end not one was found a truant in so daring a deed; all carried through their task with their dearest ones. Wretched victims of necessity, to whom to slay with their own hands their own wives and children seemed the lightest of evils. Unable, indeed, any longer to endure their anguish at what they had done, and feeling they wronged the slain by surviving them if it were but for a moment, they quickly piled together all the stores and set them on fire; then, having chosen by lot ten of their number to despatch the rest, they laid down each beside his prostrate wife and children, and, flinging their arms around them, offered their throats in readiness for the executioners of the melancholy office.

The survivors drew lots to decide which one should remain alive to the last:

> Finally, then, the nine bared their throats, and the last solitary survivor, after surveying the prostrate multitude, to see whether haply amid the shambles there were yet one left who needed his hand, and finding that all were slain, set the palace ablaze, and then collecting his strength drove his sword clean through his body and fell beside his family.

They died in the belief that they had left not a soul alive to fall into Roman hands.

The Romans broke in at daybreak, expecting the Zealots to attack them. They encountered an awesome silence. They were at a loss to understand what had happened, believing that their enemies lurked underground. From a cavern emerged two women, leading five children by the hand. One said she was a relative of Eleazar's. Josephus described her as 'superior in sagacity to most of her sex'. She told the Romans that she and the other woman had escaped the mass suicide by concealing themselves in a cave. The rest were too absorbed in their self-slaughter to notice their absence. She 'lucidly reported' Eleazar's speech and described how the deed was done. The soldiers hardly believed her story. They accepted it only when they had extinguished the flames and entered the palace. It was filled with bodies. Instead of exulting over their slain enemy, they acclaimed their nobility and contempt for death. The food in the storerooms had not all been burned; the Zealots had left some to prove that they had not given up from starvation.

For nineteen centuries, Josephus's thirdhand account of the mass suicide of the Zealots has remained our only source of information about 'one of the most dramatic episodes of Jewish history', as Professor Yadin has called it. In 1963–64 he led an archaeological expedition to the site. He described the result in his book, *Masada: Herod's Fortress and the Zealots' Last Stand*.

In one cave the archaeologists found twenty-five skeletons, those of men aged from 22 to 70, women from 15 to 22, children from 8 to 12, and the skeleton of an embryo. In the ruins of the palace there were three more. On the floor of the bath-house were discovered the skeleton of a man aged about 20 and those of a woman and child. The woman's dark brown braided hair still adhered to her scalp. The plaster of the steps on which she lay was stained with what looked like blood. In the Zealot huts were signs that life had been cut off suddenly. Pots and kettles lay strewn on the floor near the stoves. Faggots stood waiting to be ignited. Hundreds of coins came to light, both bronze and silver. They were engraved FOR THE REDEMPTION OF ZION and JERUSALEM THE HOLY. Three coins were dated THE YEAR FIVE (A.D. 70). Their presence at Masada proves a connection with beleaguered Jerusalem.

Perhaps the most poignant of all the relics were eleven potsherds. Each was inscribed with a name. They were the actual lots cast by the last survivors. One bore the name of BEN YAIR, none other than Eleazar himself.

The discovery at Masada of fragments of several scrolls was of great interest to scholars. They are identical with those found at Qumran. Their discovery revived the stormy debate about the Scrolls' original ownership. Their presence on Masada indicates either that their original owners were Zealots or that its defenders included Essenes. These scrolls were probably brought to Masada before the buildings at Qumran were overrun and destroyed by the Romans.

Excavation of the casement walls had disclosed the Zealots' methods of defence. At the strategic point overlooking the Snake Path they had piled dozens of huge round stones, each weighing some 100 pounds. They would have proved lethal to climbers. Around the western gate were clustered hundreds of *ballistae* stones, each the size of a grapefruit. These were the missiles hurled by the Roman catapults.

The fall of Masada did not completely end the Jewish revolt. Certain *Sicarii*, says Josephus, fled to Alexandria in Egypt; where, 'not content with their escape', they sought to rouse their co-religionists to assert their independence. Significantly, they employed the Zealot argument that 'they should recognize God alone as their Lord'. The Alexandrian Jewish community was

188

unmoved by this propaganda or by *Sicarii* threats. It declared itself innocent of the *Sicarii's* crimes, and denounced the dangerous fanatics to the Romans. It handed over six hundred and traced and arrested others who had escaped.

Josephus paid tribute to the courage of these *Sicarii*,

> for under every form of torture and laceration of body, devised for the sole object of making them acknowledge Caesar as Lord, not one submitted nor was brought to the verge of utterance; but all kept their resolve, triumphant over constraint, meeting the tortures and the fire with bodies that seemed insensible of pain and souls that well-nigh exalted in it. But most of all were the spectators struck by the children of tender age, not one of whom could be prevailed upon to call Caesar, Lord. So far did the strength of courage rise superior to the weakness of their frames.

Still the Jews fought for their independence. The revolt shifted to the *Diaspora*. In A.D. 110 disturbances broke out in Alexandria between Greeks and Jews. Both parties sent delegates to the Emperor Trajan, who favoured the Jews. When Trajan was occupied in war against the Parthians five years later, the Jews in Libya, Egypt, Cyrene, and Cyprus asserted their independence. They elected their own king, a man named Lykyas, and massacred the Gentile residents of these countries. The Alexandrian Greeks retaliated. They devastated the Jewish quarter of the city, killing indiscriminately. Revolts also broke out in Mesopotamia. Trajan was forced to abandon his Parthian campaign, take energetic measures, and subdue the rebellions with ruthless severity.

The Palestinian Jews revolted again in A.D. 132. They were roused beyond endurance by two Edicts issued by the Emperor Hadrian. He probably had no intention of deliberately annoying the Jews. But as a man of refined tastes he was revolted by the barbaric custom of castration, already prohibited throughout the Empire by an Edict of Domitian. Hadrian made the crime punishable by death and included circumcision in that form of mutilation. To the Jews circumcision was a divine ordinance. Its prohibition constituted a grave attack on their religion. Judaism was also threatened by the second Edict. Hadrian ordered the erection of a shrine to Jupiter on the site of the Jerusalem Temple. It had lain in ruins for sixty years and the Jews hoped one day to rebuild it.

The Romans were caught unawares by the Jewish rising. It took a different form from that of the First Revolt. This time the Jews were unanimous. They followed one leader and adopted guerilla warfare tactics, refusing to be confined in cities or to fight pitched battles.

The new leader, Simon bar Kochba, was recognized as the Messiah by a distinguished Rabbi, the Pharisee R. Akiba. Kochba neither claimed Davidic descent, thought to be an essential ingredient of Messiahship, nor claimed to perform miracles. His popularity derived from his heroism and his success. He made himself master of Judaea and set up a Jewish state. He stamped his coins SIMON THE PRINCE OF ISRAEL, and FOR THE FREEDOM OF ISRAEL.

Tinnius Rufus, the Procurator, was unable to suppress the revolt with the limited forces at his disposal. The reinforcements, when they arrived, were still insufficient. Kochba adopted the ancient Maccabean tactic. He gathered his supporters in small bands which sallied out from their strongholds, devastated the country, and returned to their hiding places. The Romans were forced to subdue each band separately. The discovery in caves near Qumran of 'despatches' written by Kochba suggest that he made that place his headquarters. The long-drawn-out war continued for three and a half years. Finally, the Roman General Julius Severus cornered and captured Kochba at Bether, near Jerusalem, his last stronghold.

The losses on both sides were again heavy. The Roman historian Dio Cassius claims that over half a million Jews died. He says that 'all Judaea was almost a wilderness'. So severe were the Roman losses that Hadrian's message to the Senate announcing the end of the war omitted the usual statement that all was well with him and his army.

The titanic struggle for national independence had ended once again in inevitable disaster.

On the desolate site of Jerusalem, Hadrian built a new city which he named Aelia Capitolina. It was laid out on the lines of a military encampment. Its straight and right-angular streets are preserved to this day. All Jews were excluded from the city on pain of death, and soon driven altogether from the Holy Land of Israel, doomed to wander the face of the earth as aliens in a heathen world. They were bound together, no longer by Temple Cultus, blood sacrifice, and fanatical religious zeal, but rather by prayer, piety, and the Law. Its study was taught at Jamnia by Jonathan ben Zakkai, according to the interpretation of the Pharisees. They were the only surviving sect of the two revolts.

The Jews survived their two national disasters. That is the stupendous fact of their history.

Twenty-one

The Fate of
the Christians

The consequences of the fall of Jerusalem to the Christians were momentous.

Like Josephus, Mark may have witnessed the Roman Triumph in A.D. 71. With the exultant shouts of the victorious Romans, and their execrations of all things Jewish, ringing in his ears, he turned to write his Gospel, his story of the foundation of the faith.

The consensus of scholarly opinion agrees that all four Gospels and the *Acts of the Apostles* were written outside Palestine for Greek-speaking readers, long after the events they record, by men who did not know Jesus and were not eyewitnesses to the scenes they describe. Mark wrote first. Matthew and Luke (the authors of *Acts* as well) wrote their Gospels about A.D. 90, and John towards the end of the century (see Moffat, *Introduction to the Literature of the New Testament*; Guignebert, *Jesus the Messiah*; Goguel, *The Birth of Christianity*).

Thus these Christian documents are considerably removed in space and time from the events they purport to record. One apparent enigma springs to our notice. Jesus and his disciples were Jews living in Palestine and speaking Aramaic, the native language. Jesus's message was addressed particularly to his own people. His followers, after his death, remained within the framework of the Jewish national religion. Yet the first accounts of his life and work, as well as the story of the progress of the movement he founded, were written outside Palestine for an alien people. This strange anomaly cannot be over-emphasized. It has been the subject of detailed inquiry.

Further examination of the Christian source documents reveal another strange fact. The Gospels and *Acts* are not the earliest known Christian documents. The letters of Paul were written twenty years before the first Gospel. When these source documents are placed in their correct chronological order—Paul, Mark, Matthew or Luke, John—a picture of the foundation and progress of the movement emerges that is very different from the one depicted in the Gospels and *Acts*. It constitutes, in the pregnant words of Professor S. G. F. Brandon (in *The Fall of Jerusalem and the Christian Church*), 'a veritable questioning of the accuracy of the generally accepted picture of Christian origins'.

Paul's letters reflect knowledge far earlier than that of the authors of the Gospels.

In the period following the Crucifixion the three 'pillars' of the movement, according to Paul, were James, Peter, and John. At first glance they are the same three men described in the Gospels as Jesus's principal lieutenants. But they are not the same and the order of precedence is different. Peter has been ousted from his position of primacy by James. He is not the James the son of Zebedee of the Gospels, but James 'the brother of the Lord', Jesus's sceptical and antagonistic relative. He became the acknowledged and revered leader of the movement. This man of Jesus's own kin institutes a family Caliphate. He is succeeded on his death by a nephew of Jesus, named Symeon.

Extraordinary as is this revelation, an even more amazing one requires notice.

The *Acts of the Apostles*, the story of the progress of the movement after Jesus's Crucifixion, presents an idyllic picture in which the new faith is finally carried to Rome by Paul, with 'none forbidding'. Paul, self-appointed Apostle to the Gentiles, and the original disciples argue amicably on the question of the admission of non-Jews without the necessity for circumcision. According to *Acts* the dispute is finally settled in Paul's favour, and at an Apostolic Council held in Jerusalem he is accorded a decision absolving Gentile converts from all but minor requirements of the Jewish Law. This decision is embodied in a decree issued to all the churches.

But Paul's own letters, written while the controversy was at its height, indicate that there was no such decree made in his favour and that his dispute with the men who had known Jesus went far deeper, affecting the very fundamentals of the faith.

As Dr F. C. Baur (*in Paul, His Life and Works*) first remarked, there is not in Paul's writings 'the slightest suggestion that such an important decree had been made at that time, but rather the most decided assurances to the contrary'. In his *Epistle to the Galatians*, written shortly after his visit to Jerusalem, Paul does not cite the decree. If it existed it would have provided the Apostolic support, which he so fervently desired, for his authority and teaching.

Paul's letters, written half a century before *Acts*, reveal that within twenty years of the Crucifixion of Jesus the movement he had founded was rent by fierce strife. The conflict between Paul and the Mother Church at Jerusalem concerned nothing less than the fundamental beliefs of the new faith and centred around two rival interpretations of the nature and mission of Jesus. *Acts* obscures this bitter quarrel and reverses its result.

Paul shows himself resisting and combating opponents of great prestige and unchallengeable authority, the men who had walked and talked with Jesus. He describes them as preaching '*another* Jesus' and setting forth a '*different* Gospel'. He calls his opponents 'servants of Satan', 'false prophets', 'spurious brethren', and 'false beguilers'. They had penetrated into his own specially chosen missionary field to combat his doctrines.

By the word Gospel in this context Paul means the fundamental concepts of Christianity—the basic beliefs about Jesus, his nature and mission. This Bible 'detection' is important in discussion of Christian origins.

The Gospels and *Acts* reflect the beliefs of second-generation Christians *at the time when they were written*, half a century or so *after* the Crucifixion. In order to learn what were the original beliefs we need to try to discover the state of mind of the men who actually knew Jesus. This is an intricate problem, because, save for a few words recorded early in *Acts*, no documents have survived which explain the beliefs of the original disciples immediately after the Crucifixion, at the time when they were disputing with Paul.

The authors of the Gospels drew their material from traditions they received from Palestine *after* the Mother Church at Jerusalem, and its leaders, had been wiped out in the fall and destruction of the city. Paul had also disappeared from the scene. Before he 'appealed to Caesar' and was sent to Rome for trial, Paul acknowledged the supremacy and authority of the leaders of the Church of Jerusalem and his own defeat. Yet the Gospels reflect theologically not the beliefs of the original disciples and Jesus's own brother but the discredited and defeated doctrines of Paul, their opponent, whose beliefs survived him.

It was an extraordinary reversal of the situation we might reasonably expect, but a logical one when we trace the reason for it.

The true origin of Christianity cannot be understood without explanation of the situation which led to the writing of the Gospels. Two major factors influenced their authors: the outcome of the conflict between Paul and the original Apostles, and the destruction of Jerusalem, which crushed the revolt of the Jews.

That primitive Christianity was rent by this fierce conflict was first detected by Dr F. C. Baur. Its full significance in relation to the fall of Jerusalem, and the impact of both on the authors of the Gospels, has only recently been explained by Professor S. G. F. Brandon, without whose careful investigation the whole question of Christian origins would have remained a morass of misunderstanding.

The kernel of the conflict was Jesus's supposed nature and mission. Paul, the newcomer, a man who did not profess to have known Jesus 'in the flesh', saw him as the divine and pre-existent Son of God. Paul had no interest in Jesus as the Jewish Messiah, no interest in his Crucifixion. But his Resurrection was a startling manifestation of the age-old myth of the dying and resuscitated God, well known in the East at that time. Paul appears embarrassed by knowledge of the historic Jesus, the man who had so recently been executed by the Romans for treason. To Paul the risen Jesus was the long expected World Saviour, more real than Mithras, Dionysus, Adonis, or Osiris. He tried to convert the Apostles and Jesus's brother to his view. They, on the other hand, saw Jesus as the promised Jewish Messiah, 'a man sent by God', who on his return to the world would 'restore the kingdom to Israel'. Paul's conception of Jesus's unique relationship to God

—his 'divinity'—was, as Professor Brandon points out, completely unknown in contemporary Jewish thought, which placed an absolute gulf between God and man.

The abyss which stood between Paul and James, the 'brother of the Lord'—who, though head of the Christian Church, was also an orthodox Jew worshipping the God of the Jews in the Temple—constituted nothing less than the difference between God and man. In orthodox Jewish thought all Jews were in a sense 'sons of God', but the Messiah was not divine. The question between the two rival Christian parties was which professed the true and which the false Christianity.

Paul had the temerity to tell James that his brother, born of his own parents, the boy he had played with in the streets of Nazareth, was the incarnated Son of God, the pre-existent Christ who had taken human form, a belief deeply repugnant to orthodox Jews, as we have seen.

Paul, a Jew from Tarsus, a city in Cilicia, Asia Minor, was, he tells us, educated in Jerusalem as a disciple of the Pharisee Gamaliel. Paul appears first in Christian literature as a self-styled but peculiarly passive persecutor of the faith. Suddenly converted by a vision on the road to Damascus, he travelled to Jerusalem to meet James, Peter, and John. He then appointed himself a special missionary to the Gentiles.

The Jewish Christians could not allow Paul to use their movement as a vehicle for his un-Jewish ideas. Their propagation would bring upon Jewish Christians the wrath of their countrymen, the very men they wished to convert to the belief that Jesus, despite his Crucifixion, was still the promised Messiah. From the Clementine *Recognitions*—third-century Christian writings based on Palestinian tradition—comes a reflection of this conflict. According to this source, Peter charged the brethren at Tripolis to believe no teacher unless he brought with him the testimonial of James the Lord's brother, and he warned them against 'false prophets and false Apostles and false teachers, who indeed speak in the name of Christ, but do the work of the devil'.

Paul knew that in the final showdown he must bow to the impregnable position of his opponents. They and not he had been Jesus's friends. After his own teaching and authority had been repudiated, Paul journeyed to Jerusalem hoping to obtain some official sanction for his position, but with trepidation and misgivings, 'not knowing the things that shall befall me there'.

The 'grievous wolves' Paul so much feared—James and the Apostles—disposed of Paul with subtlety. They accused him of teaching his converts to reject the national religion and invited him to prove his Jewish orthodoxy by submitting to a test in the presence of his own converts. This stratagem would either prove his 'adherence' to Jewish custom, and consequently shatter his authority with his own Gentile converts, or result in his public expulsion from the movement. In this crucial dilemma, Paul chose to submit to the test, ceding victory to his powerful opponents.

While in the Temple performing the Nazarite Vow, the ritual required to demonstrate his orthodoxy, Paul was observed by certain Jews from Asia Minor who were acquainted with his unorthodox beliefs. They accused him of taking a Gentile into the Temple precincts, a capital crime. He was attacked as a law-breaker by the mob, from whom he was rescued by the Roman guards. As a Roman citizen he appealed to Caesar and was eventually sent to Rome for trial. Paul's discomfiture and arrest solved the difficulty within the movement.

Paul's fate is unrecorded. But if he was finally set at liberty it is inconceivable that the author of *Acts* should pass over in utter silence an event for which the reader had been prepared. Paul's unorthodox beliefs had been decisively rejected. Yet within twenty years they were generally accepted as Christian doctrine. Only the complete disappearance of one party to the dispute could have left the way open for the revival of the discredited beliefs of the other. This extraordinary reversal was due to an event which changed completely the whole course of the Christian movement.

Fifteen years after Paul's defeat, the Mother Church at Jerusalem—the Apostolic Body hitherto the paramount and recognized front of Christian authority—was annihilated in the destruction of Jerusalem and the crushing defeat of the Jewish nationalists. The Christian Messianist movement had, in the words of Professor Brandon, 'identified itself too closely with the aspirations of its own nation and it shared its annihilation'.

How did Christianity record this event of epoch-making consequence to itself?

The answer is by silence, complete and absolute. The fall of Jerusalem, the destruction of its sacred Temple, Holy Sanctuary of both Judaism and Christianity; the collapse and disappearance of the Apostolic Body, hitherto the supreme authority and symbol of Christian prestige; and the fate of the original followers of Jesus went unrecorded in Christian literature until the fourth century. The books of the New Testament ignore it. Thus did the later Christians draw the veil of silence over the Church's embarrassing past.

The reason for the reversal, then, was that Paul's beliefs were far more acceptable to Gentiles than the Jewish conception of Jesus as Messiah-King. With the failure of Jesus to come to his people's rescue at the moment of national crisis, Jewish interest waned and Jewish Christianity came to its inevitable end. Jesus ceased to be a Jewish national hero. But among Christians the crucified leader of an abortive revolt became the Son of God, even God Himself. Paul's Christianity provided the basis for a new, largely Gentile religion of worldwide validity. The triumph of the Apostolic Body had been short-lived.

For a time the nationalistic beliefs of the original followers of Jesus survived in the Church of Alexandria in Egypt, to which some survivors of the national disaster had succeeded in escaping, and among the small Christian Jewish communities which lingered on in parts of Palestine for four hundred years. But for the disaster of A.D. 70, the movement founded by Jesus might have continued as an offshoot of Judaism and been finally re-absorbed within it.

The other factor which influenced the Evangelists, particularly Mark, was the hatred of the Romans for all things Jewish after the revolt of the Jews.

The comparative lateness of the appearance of the four biographical accounts of part of Jesus's life is often attributed to the primitive expectation of the imminent return of Jesus and the end of the world. When after a time this did not materialize, lives of Jesus, it is said, were required to preserve the re-collections of those who had known him. But Mark's Gospel was a revolutionary innovation, an unprecedented departure from Christian practice clearly called into being by some event of notable significance. Mark's apologia is directed to meet the situation arising from the defeat of the Jewish national cause.

Mark had three purposes in mind: to preserve the Palestinian traditions derived from the now defunct Mother Church, to revive Paul's interpretation of Christianity—now possible after the disappearance of his victorious opponents—and, above all, to overcome Roman hostility to a movement which had been closely identified with the cause of Jewish freedom.

To the Gentile Christians outside Palestine the fate of their Jewish brethren had been most embarrassing. In the eyes of the Romans, in whose world they had to live, the Christian Messianists, Jewish and Gentile, were linked with the Zealots as the instigators of the revolt which had cost the Romans so much blood and money to crush.

The Romans viewed Christianity and Christians as a 'dangerous superstition', 'those hated for their abominations', 'those who made great tumult in Rome', 'abettors of a pest which threatens the whole world', 'they who have turned the world upside down', 'men who did not obey the laws of Caesar, saying "there is another King, one Jesus"'. Josephus, as we have seen, considered Christianity to be a revolutionary movement against Rome. Sulpicius Severus preserves the tradition that Titus ordered the destruction of the Temple because it was a source of revolutionary inspiration to the Christians as well as to the Jews.

These Roman opinions about Christianity are most suggestive. Since the Romans traditionally tolerated all religions, it can be inferred only that they considered the Christian Messianists dangerous political agitators in the Jewish nationalistic cause.

To ensure the survival of Gentile Christianity by overcoming Roman hostility it was necessary to convince the Romans that the new faith, though Jewish in origin, had nothing in common with the recently defeated Jewish nationalist cause. To explain this the Christians faced a peculiar difficulty. Their founder had been put to death by the Romans not many years before as a claimant to the Jewish throne, the Messiah-King, the embodiment of nationalistic hopes. Therefore he must now be depicted as a harmless religious visionary and dissociated from his racial and national background. The writing of such a book had become most urgent.

So Mark set out to shift the blame for the death of Jesus to the shoulders of the leaders of his own nation, portraying the Jews as the bitter enemies of Christ. The trumped-up charge on which Jesus had been convicted as a usurper king became a Jewish lie: the Jewish leaders, fearing Jesus's influence with the people, had persuaded Pilate to execute him on a false charge of treason. For Mark to accept Jesus as the long-awaited Jewish Messiah would have been to admit that he was indeed guilty of treason against the Romans. Mark showed Jesus, therefore, not as a claimant to political kingship but as the long-awaited World Saviour, rejected by his own nation.

How Mark set out to achieve his apologetic purpose is evident from the way in which he handles his material. For example, he repudiates Jesus's Davidic descent, to which Paul, writing twenty years earlier (*Romans* 1:3) had borne witness. Why? Because descent from the Warrior King David was a distinctive feature of the Messianic claim. Elsewhere Mark twists the incident of the provocative question about the tribute money to imply that Jesus had prudently avoided involvement in a dangerous political issue. He disguises, too, the true identity of one of Jesus's intimate band.

How well Mark succeeded in his propaganda to free the Christians from the stigma of Jewish Messianism is evident. Towards the end of the century the Emperor Domitian, in an attempt to stamp out Messianism, caused those who claimed Davidic descent to be rounded up. Two grandsons of Jude (another of Jesus's brothers) named James and Zokher were arrested and brought to Rome. They were interrogated by Domitian. The later Christian writer Hegesippus (here quoted by Eusebius) describes the occasion:

He put the question whether they were of David's race, and they confessed that they were. He then asked them what

200

property they had, or how much money they possessed, and both of them answered that they had between them only nine thousand denarii, and this they had not in silver, but in the value of a piece of land containing only thirty-nine acres; from which they raised their taxes and supported themselves by their own labour. Then they also began to show their hands, exhibiting the hardness of their bodies, and the callosity formed by incessant labour on their hands, as evidence of their own labour. When asked, also, respecting the Messiah and his kingdom, what was its nature, and when and where it was to appear, they replied, that it was not a temporal nor an earthly kingdom, but celestial and angelic; that it would appear at the end of the world, when coming in glory he would judge the living and the dead, and give to everyone according to his works. Upon which Domitian, despising them, made no reply; but treating them with contempt as simpletons commanded them to be dismissed, and by a decree ordered the persecution to cease. (Eusebius, *Ecclesiastica Historica*)

Other Christians, according to the third-century Roman historian Dio Cassius, were punished for denying the Roman gods. This alleged atheism was found to extend to within the Emperor's own family, some members of which were probably Gentile Christians of Paul's persuasion. The famous correspondence between the Emperor Trajan and the younger Pliny shows that Christians were technically 'outlaws'—members of an illegal association. But there was now no inclination to persecute them as long as they conformed to Roman law. That individuals were pardoned on recantation proves that they were no longer considered a threat to the security of the State.

Its Messianic hope unfulfilled, the Mother Church of Jerusalem had disappeared with the fall and destruction of the city. The results, then, of the siege and fall of Jerusalem on the later history of the Western world are incalculable. Had the Mother Church not fallen, its Messianic hope unfulfilled, Christianity as we know it might have been suppressed before it ever flowered.

Appendix A

The
Slavonic Josephus

Virtually unknown outside a select group of scholars, a bitter controversy has raged for a hundred years about the value of certain manuscripts attributed to the Jewish historian Josephus, written in the old Slavonic tongue, which have been found in Russia. They comprise a mystery which, if it could be solved to everyone's satisfaction, might finally elucidate one of the greatest problems left by the Gospel: Was Jesus a political agitator and a revolutionary?

The standard texts of Josephus's *Jewish War* contain no reference to Jesus or to the early Christians. This is a remarkable omission in the light of many pagan references which indicate that the Romans believed the Christians to be the motivators, with the Zealots, of the Revolt of the Jews. Certain scholars claim that Josephus did write about Jesus, and that his hostile passage was suppressed when the early Christians became sufficiently powerful to censor documents which differed from the Gospels. Powers to censor and suppress all writings hostile to Christianity were accorded by the Emperor Constantine after A.D. 325. They were re-enacted by the Emperors Theodosius II (A.D. 408–450) and Valentinian III (A.D. 425–455) after the pagan revival by the Emperor Julian the Apostate.

The *Codex Justinianus* contains the order of these Emperors for the burning of many books. The death penalty was imposed for the possession of works which described Jesus as a 'magician', 'agitator', or 'revolutionary'. That so little information is supplied by pagan authors is proof of the wide application of these powers. This paucity has given rise to the theory that Jesus was a figment of his biographers' imaginations.

The Christian censors who set out to remove Josephus's damaging remarks, and to turn him into a witness for the truths of Christianity, may have slipped up. Certain manuscripts of his *Jewish War* eluded their vigilance, or so it seems.

Sixteen 'manuscripts of Josephus' found in Russia in 1866 were noticed to be different from the usual Greek texts of his works. They were shorter and contained some remarkable deviations and additions. Among these are three references to John the Baptist, Jesus, and the early Christians.

Josephus's first publication was intended as a warning to Eastern peoples of the dangers of rebellion against Rome. He achieved this in his own language, Aramaic, the common tongue of the Semitic world including Palestine. This version was entitled, *On the Capture of Jerusalem*.

To achieve his second purpose of writing the official history, a version in Greek—common language of the Roman world—was needed. Josephus himself was but a poor Greek scholar and he could only carry his work to the stage of a rough and literal translation from the Aramaic. From that his Greek assistants prepared a polished Greek text entitled (from the Roman point of view) *The Jewish War*. This finished Greek text was published in successive editions between A.D. 75 and 79, following an earlier but shorter edition that appeared in time for the Emperor's Triumph in A.D. 71.

The texts of the Aramaic and the Greek versions were not the same, and the different titles used imply a different treatment for different purposes.

The book was ordered to be placed in public libraries throughout the Empire. Josephus had been given access to the Imperial Archives, to the Reports of the Roman Governors, and to the Commentaries of the Julian and Claudian Emperors, as well as to the campaign diaries of Vespasian and Titus. Critical examination of the text of his work demonstrates the sections where these official records were incorporated verbatim.

Yet, according to the standard texts of his work, Josephus knew nothing about Jesus, whereas he duly records the Messianic careers of Judas of Galilee and Theudas and others. Even more curious is the complete absence from his book of any mention of the fire of Rome in A.D. 64, when he himself was in that city. These omissions suggest that a complete chapter has been removed.

It seems probable that Josephus found reference to Jesus in the Roman Archives. Provincial governors were required to send reports, and no important trial, particularly when the accusation was treason against the Emperor, could have been conducted without a report justifying the verdict. Such a procedure would certainly have been followed in a case in which a man had been tried as a usurper king, a rival to Caesar himself, in a province noted for its turbulence. Particularly so during the reign of the Emperor Tiberius, who insisted on being kept informed of even the most trivial incidents. Both Justin Martyr and Tertullian, Christian writers of the second and third centuries, presumed that an account of the trial of Jesus existed in the Roman Archives. It would have been quite possible for early Christians, even the writers of the Gospels, to have obtained copies. That they did not suggests that the record did justify the verdict.

In his history, up to the death of Herod the Great in 4 B.C. and perhaps up to A.D. 6, when Judaea became a Roman province, Josephus drew upon the work of Nicholas of Damascus, a Greek official of Herod's Court and the author of a *Universal History* in 144 books, which were subsequently lost.

Josephus's own recollection of current events commenced about the year A.D. 60, when he was twenty-two years of age. For the intervening years he relied upon the official records obtainable in Rome. For this period of fifty-four years the text of his work is characteristic of such material and lacks intimate detail.

From the time when Judaea became a Roman province to the re-establishment of the monarchy by Agrippa I, the official nature of the work is evident. Many passages are little more than a transcription of official reports. During the short period of Agrippa's reign (A.D. 41–44) Josephus shows lack of knowledge of events, but with the return of the Procurators and the renewal of their reports to Rome the documentary nature of his history recommences.

For example, Josephus quotes the will of Herod the Great; the speeches at the investigation conducted by the Emperor

Augustus into the claims of Herod's sons and the counter-claims of the Jewish delegation; the petition of the Jews which led to the banishment of Archelaus; and the Proclamation annexing his territory as an imperial province. The tumults of the governorship of Pilate are based on the extracts from the Procurator's official diary, the *Acta Pilati*.

The statement of Eusebius, who published his *History of the Church* in A.D. 325, proves that the *Acta Pilati*, which reported Jesus's trial, was published in A.D. 311 by the order of the Emperor Maximianus in order to counteract Christian propaganda. It was immediately suppressed when the Church was given authority to censor such documents. Eusebius claimed that the *Acta* was a forgery because it dated the trial differently from the date implied by Luke; he did not deny that a report of the trial existed.

After the recall of Pilate, the official character of Josephus's work continues; for example, the exact date of the death of the Emperor Tiberius is given; the document naming Agrippa Tetrarch of Philip's territories is quoted; Agrippa's accusations against Antipas and his banishment are recorded.

The fact that no official records were available in Rome for the period of the reign of Agrippa I accounts for the absence of information about his persecution of the Christians. It involved the execution of James, and possibly of John, the sons of Zebedee, as well as the imprisonment of Peter.

The documentary basis of his history resumes when the Procurators returned on Agrippa I's death in A.D. 44, and Josephus's own recollections of events in Palestine start in A.D. 60 and continue, except for an intermission when he was in Rome for two years. For the war which broke out in A.D. 66 the campaign diaries of Vespasian and his generals are freely drawn upon. Many military details could only have been acquired from such sources.

It is unlikely that Josephus omitted reference to Jesus and the Christians. He believed that the 'Messianists', with the Zealots, had caused the downfall of the Jews by precipitating a hopeless war against Rome.

If, as certain scholars think, the Slavonic additions are derived from Josephus's original work, before it was fully censored, the historian referred to Jesus in uncomplimentary terms, as might be expected from an author of his religious and political background.

The Slavonic manuscripts of Josephus are entitled *On the Capture of Jerusalem*, the title of the historian's original Aramaic version, not *Concerning the Jewish War*, the title of the later Greek edition. The name of the author is given simply as 'Josephus', without the addition of his Roman family name, 'Flavius'.

The text of the Aramaic version was shorter because it was published before events incorporated in later editions had happened. This shorter and earlier version formed the original from which the Slavonic manuscripts are derived.

The deviations and additions found in the Slavonic texts particularly refer to John the Baptist, Jesus, and the early Christians, though there are also many other additions unrelated to Christianity. They provide information which could only have been known to a contemporary historian.

Examination of these manuscripts indicate that they were derived from a rough Greek translation of Josephus's original Aramaic version entitled *On the Capture of Jerusalem*. This translation was prepared by the author for the use of his Greek assistants who were unable to translate Aramaic directly into the polished Greek from which the standard texts of today are derived. That the Slavonic manuscripts are derived from a Greek original is clear, but a number of Semiticisms which have been removed from the polished Greek version still remain.

The Slavonic manuscripts commence in the same way as the standard Greek text. Their ending show that they were derived from an older and simpler draft brought up to the year A.D. 75 only. They are thus based on the second edition of the work, rather than the first, which was even shorter and hurriedly prepared for the Emperor's Triumph in A.D. 71.

The Slavonic manuscripts are not without Christian changes and alterations, derived from the Greek manuscripts employed in their translation. This shows that certain anti-Christian passages were only removed from the original Greek texts after this translation had been made.

The translation from Greek to Old Russian, some scholars believe, took place in Lithuania between A.D. 1250 and 1261. The translator, a heretic priest, worked from two different manuscripts starting with one from which a certain number of copies were circulated and then acquiring a better one from which further copies were made. The Greek texts used were of Byzantine origin copied in Asia Minor between A.D. 1204 and 1261. Their place of origin can be inferred from the use of the expressions 'Italians' and 'Latins' to denote the people of the Empire of the West.

This Old Russian translation of Josephus's work was prepared for a heretic sect, which flourished in Russia in the thirteenth century. It was used in the denial of the divinity of Jesus. Thus even as altered by the Christians, Josephus could still be quoted as a supporter of these views. The fact that the Slavonic manuscripts contain many Christian rewordings today shows that they were not prepared by an orthodox Jew, who would have omitted them. Such an anti-Christian forgery, requiring the rewriting of an entire Josephus text with a few minor alterations, would have been pointless.

This 'Jewish' heresy was originally derived from certain Jewish Christians who survived in the deserts of Northern Arabia and Mesopotamia for some centuries. They refused to accept the divine origin of Jesus, regarding him as a prophet. Their converts became known as the 'Josephinists'. The sect spread into northern Italy and Provence. They owned the works of Josephus in a form partly free from the censorship which otherwise turned his works into a witness for orthodox Christianity and rendered them acceptable for the Canon of several Eastern Churches. The discovery by the Church that there were still in circulation manuscripts of Josephus at variance with the Gospel story in that they revealed a revolutionary past led to the complete deletion of all passages referring to Jesus and the Baptist. Only the Josephinists remained in possession of texts descended from the Aramaic version of *The Capture of Jerusalem* in which the passages dealing with Jesus and the Baptist survived. Their sect, carrying their partly unexpurgated text of Josephus, spread to South Russia.

Dr Robert Eisler (*The Messiah Jesus and John the Baptist*) has traced the progress of this heresy in Russia. The Khazars, a South Russian people of Turkish origin, adopted Judaism as their state religion. On their overthrow by the Russians in A.D. 967, they were forced to become converts to Christianity. As a result their descendants were easily affected by the Judaizing heresy three hundred years later.

The heresy spread from the Crimea within the Russian Orthodox Church, reaching even into the family of the Czar, before it was suppressed. It was through this sect that the Greek manuscripts of Josephus were acquired from the parent body in Asia Minor. It is only in the places in Russia where these heretics lived, or to which they were banished, that the Slavonic manuscripts have been found.

Dr Eisler has explained his reasons for presuming that these Slavonic manuscripts are ultimately derived from Josephus's original Aramaic version of *The Capture of Jerusalem*. No satisfactory alternative has been advanced. Comparisons of the passages relating to Josephus's actions while he was in command in Galilee demonstrate that the additions found in the Slavonic texts could only have come from the pen of Josephus himself. A number of additions refer to other matters. Of these, one is of particular significance in relation to the authenticity of these texts.

In the standard version of *The Jewish War* there is a short account of the Battle of Bedriacum in Gaul in A.D. 69. The passage in the Slavonic is far longer, and it contains a description of a particular strategy of which there is no mention by any other historian. This is in the use of three-pronged irons strewn on the ground to lame horses. The two passages read:

THE JEWISH WAR

In the battle fought at Bedriacum in Gaul, against Valens and Caccina, the generals of Vitelius, on the first day Otho

SLAVONIC TEXT

On the first day Otho was victor but on the second Vitelius. For he had during the night strewn the ground with had the advantage, but on the second the troops of Vitelius.

three-pronged irons. And in the morning, after they had drawn up in order of battle, when Vitelius feigned flight Otho pursued after them with his troops. And they reached the place on which the irons were strewn. Then were the horses lamed, and it was impossible either for the horses or for the men to extricate themselves. And the soldiers of Vitelius who had turned back slew all who lay there. But Otho saw what had befallen and killed himself.

Opponents of Eisler's theory suggest that the Slavonic texts are medieval forgeries, either Christian or Jewish, designed to turn Josephus into a witness for or against Christ. The fact that two such contrary suggestions are made indicates the difficulty in supplying an alternative derivation. If these texts are forgeries, it means either a Christian or a Jewish scribe went to the enormous labour of copying out by hand the entire text of Josephus purely in order to insert three short additions, which, as they stand, do nothing either to substantiate or deny the truths of Christianity, which at that time no one questioned. Why did not the supposed Christian scribe attempt to parallel the Gospel story? How is it that the supposed Jewish scribe allowed obvious Christian interpolations to remain in the text? How could either have known about the three-pronged irons of the battle of Bedriacum, a detail which could only have been drawn from a report of that battle by a contemporary historian, such as Josephus, who had access to such reports?

In their present form, without interpretation, the Slavonic additions relating to Christianity are meaningless. Imaginative reconstruction was necessary to restore them to the form in which Josephus originally wrote them. This Dr Eisler has done.

In the opinion of many scholars, he has gone too far. Many of his doubtful additions, culled from quotations he believed other authors had extracted before Josephus's works were censored, can be ignored. Three passages refer to John the Baptist, James, and the early Christians. John and Jesus are called, respectively, the 'Wild Man' and the 'Wonder-Worker'.

The first passage implies that John's mission was political in nature. He demands, in A.D. 6, the overthrow of Roman rule and the installation of a native king. He is put to death about the year A.D. 35 by Herod Antipas, for fear that his teaching might lead to insurrection.

The Slavonic passage relating to Jesus reads as follows:

At the time there appeared a man, if it is permissible to call him a man. His nature (and form) were human, but his appearance (was something) more than (that) of a man; (notwithstanding his works were divine). He worked miracles wonderful and mighty. (Therefore it is impossible for me to call him a man); but again, if I look at the nature which he shared with all, I will not call him an angel. And everything whatsoever he wrought through an invisible power, he wrought by word and command. Some said of him: 'Our first law-giver is risen from the dead and hath performed many healings and arts,' while others thought he was sent from God. Howbeit in many things he disobeyed the Law and kept not the Sabbath according to (our) fathers' customs. Yet, on the other hand, he did nothing shameful; nor (did he do anything) with aid of hands, but by words alone did he provide everything.

And many of the multitude followed after him and hearkened to his teachings; and many souls were in commotion thinking that thereby the Jewish tribes might free themselves from Roman hands. Now it was his custom in general to sojourn over against the city upon the Mount of Olives, and there, too, he bestowed his healings upon the people.

And there assembled unto him of ministers one hundred and fifty, and a multitude of the people. Now when they saw his power, that he accomplished whatsoever he would by (a) word, and when they had made known to him their will, that he should enter into the city and cut down the Roman troops and Pilate and rule over us, he disdained us not.

And when thereafter knowledge of it came to the Jewish leaders they assembled together with the high-priest and spake: 'We are powerless and (too) weak to withstand the Romans. Seeing, moreover, that the bow is bent, we will go and communicate to Pilate that we have heard and we shall be clear of trouble, lest he hear (it) from others, and we be robbed of our substance and ourselves slaughtered and our children scattered.' And they went and communicated (it) to Pilate. And he sent and had many of the multitude slain. And he had that Wonder-Worker brought up, and after instituting an inquiry concerning him, he pronounced judgment: 'He is (a benefactor not) a malefactor, (nor) a rebel, (nor) covetous of Kingship.' (And he let him go for he had healed his dying wife.)

And he went to his wonted place and did his wonted works. And when more people again assembled round him, he glorified himself through his actions more than all. The doctors of the Law were overcome with envy, and gave thirty talents to Pilate, in order that he should put him to death. And he took (it) and gave them liberty to execute their will themselves. And they laid their hands on him and crucified him contrary to the law of (their) fathers.

This passage as is stands is marred by Christian interpolations shown here in parentheses—as, for example, the legend that Jesus healed Pilate's wife. It is not as Josephus wrote it. Dr Eisler rationalizes the author's words:

And many of the multitude followed after him and accepted his teaching, and many souls were excited thinking that thereby the Jewish tribes might be freed from Roman hands. But it was his custom most of the time to abide over against the city on the Mount of Olives, and there too he bestowed his healings upon the people. And there assembled unto him of helpers one hundred and fifty and a multitude of the mob.

And when they saw his power, how he accomplished whatsoever he would by a magic word, and when they had made known to him their will, that he should enter into the city, cut down the Roman troops and Pilate and rule over us, he disdained them not.

And when thereafter knowledge of it came to the Jewish leaders, they assembled together with the High Priest and spake: 'We are powerless and too weak to withstand the Romans. But seeing the bow is bent, we will go and impart to Pilate what we have heard, and we shall be safe, lest he hear of it from others and we be robbed of our substance and ourselves slaughtered and the Children of Israel dispersed.' And they went and imparted the matter to Pilate and he sent and had many of the multitude slain. And he had that Wonder-Worker brought up, and after instituting an inquiry concerning him, he passed sentence upon him: 'He is a malefactor, a rebel, a robber thirsting for the crown.' And they took him and crucified him according to the custom of their fathers.

In another Slavonic manuscript, when Jesus is invited to 'rule over us' we read that he 'did not heed it'. This seems to parallel his action, recorded in the Fourth Gospel, of withdrawing when he saw that the people intended to make him king by force. The suggestion that Jesus was crucified by the Jews is a reflection, inserted by the Christian censors, of the Gospel attempt to throw the blame for Jesus's death onto the Jews. Dr Eisler thinks that, following the words 'he disdained them not', Josephus added the statement, 'and having all flocked into Jerusalem they raised an uproar, uttering blasphemies against God and Caesar'. Dr Eisler recovered these words from the Chronicle of John of Antioch, written about A.D. 620. He believes that John found them in an unexpurgated manuscript of Josephus. By the removal of this passage from Josephus's text, the Christian censors turned an actual outbreak into a plan of revolt. They did that to conform with the Gospels which sought to explain Jesus's arrest as a precaution to prevent such an outbreak.

This passage precedes the description of the disturbance in Jerusalem as recorded in the standard text of Josephus. The disturbances were occasioned by Pilate's attempt to seize the Temple funds in order to pay for an aqueduct. Significantly, the standard text refers to this occasion as the 'second outbreak', implying an earlier one. Of it there is no mention, because, apparently, the passage about Jesus had been deleted.

If Dr Eisler's restoration of Josephus's original text is correct, we have there an account of the arrival of Jesus in Jerusalem which is significantly missing from the standard Greek text. In the words of Professor Brandon (*The Fall of Jerusalem and the Christian Church*), the most striking feature is 'the fact that the chief significance of the career of the Wonder-Worker (and the subsequent activity of his followers) is regarded as political'. His words excite political desire for national emancipation from Rome; he is specially invited to lead an armed attempt to overthrow the Roman government; and he is finally executed as a rebel by Pilate after the forceful suppression of his followers. The only doubt, as Professor Brandon points out, is whether he accepted or disdained the demand that he lead an armed revolt. Professor Brandon finds great importance in the fact that the Jewish historian recognized Christianity primarily as a revolutionary movement against Rome, 'for it means that to an external and unsympathetic observer the new faith must have presented such features that he was led to depict it as political in inspiration and intent rather than under any other guise'.

The third Slavonic addition refers to the activities of followers of the Wonder-Worker during the reign of the Emperor Claudius, between the years A.D. 44 and 48. This passage implies that the Christians were teaching that their Master, 'who was alive though he had been dead', was still able to free his people from the Roman yoke. The expression 'alive though he was dead' is just such a clumsy version of the Resurrection story as might have been employed by some Roman official, to whom the idea of a person rising from the dead was incomprehensible and from whose report Josephus copied it.

The other three minor additions refer to certain signs and wonders at the Resurrection. There is an account, for example, of an inscription placed in the Temple declaring that Jesus, 'the king who did not reign, was crucified by the Jews because he foretold the end of the city and the utter destruction of the Temple'. (This seems to reflect the belief that Jesus was considered by the Jews to be a violator of the Laws of Moses.) And there is a statement that some took the prophecy of the coming of the World Ruler to refer to King Herod the Great, others to the crucified Messiah, and still others to the Emperor Vespasian.

Dr Eisler's reconstruction of the Slavonic passages has not gone without violent opposition from orthodox scholars, led by Dr J. W. Jack (*The Historic Jesus*). On the other hand, scholars of the repute of Dr S. Reinach, H. St J. Thackeray, and Professor S. F. G. Brandon except his general theory that the passages are derived from the historian's original work.

Overmuch cannot be made of these Slavonic additions. They may represent views of an unsympathetic observer. Their importance lies in the confirmation they provide for the statements of the Roman historians, and for hints found in the Gospels that Jesus's career had political motivation.

Appendix B

The Habakkuk
Commentary

Menahem is identified by Professors C. Roth and G. R. Driver as the Teacher of Righteousness who, as described in the *Habakkuk Commentary*, is destroyed by the Wicked Priest (Eleazar?) on or near to the Day of Atonement. There are many points of similarity, they claim, between Josephus's narrative and the wording of the *Commentary*.

Habakkuk Commentary	*Josephus-Jewish War*
An unnamed Rightful Teacher with Messianic aspirations pursued 'to the place where he was discovered'	Menahem described as a 'sophist "decked in royal atire" hunted into the open.'
with intent 'to swallow him up' by an unnamed Wicked Priest 'whose heart was lifted up' when he took office	and murdered on Mt. Opel by Eleazar son of the high-priest 'a very rash young man' and 'acting as captain of the Temple
on 'their' Day of Atonement, during a 'Kittian' invasion; the 'house' or party of Absalom treacherously failing to help the Teacher,	near the beginning of Tishri during the war with Rome; Absalom and other followers, while trying secretly to escape,
'silenced' or 'destroyed' and	massacred and

the 'house of Judah'   Judah's grandson, Eleazar ben
                                 Jair, with a few followers

saved by God.   saved by a 'stealthy' flight.

The coincidence of two such episodes occurring in Jerusalem
on or near the Day of Atonement (depending on the differences
between the Legal and Zealot calendars) at the time of a war
against foreigners would be, these scholars claim, remarkable.
Professor Driver further identifies two other characters described
in the Scrolls. The 'Man of Falsehood' fits Josephus's description
of John of Gischala as a crafty and an unscrupulous intriguer,
and the 'Lion of Wrath' may have identified Simon Gioras,
whom Josephus describes as raging like 'a wounded beast'.

Thus, if Professors Roth and Driver are correct, the Zealots
had made Qumran their stronghold in A.D. 6, and members of
their sect wrote the Scrolls, probably between the years A.D. 68
and 73, when Professor Driver believes their stronghold was
overrun by the Romans. The survivors escaped to Masada. Con-
vincing and attractive as is the theory of Zealot ownership, the
texts of the Scrolls are so obscure to all but scholars in that field
that they add little to our detailed knowledge of the great revolt
of the Jews, which they may mirror. If their original ownership
could be definitely established, they might well enlarge our
knowledge of Zealot beliefs.

Bibliography

Ancient Sources:

Claudius, Imperator. *Letter to Alexandrians in Select Papirri.* Translated by A. S. Hunt and C. C. Edgar, Loeb Classical Library, Vol. II, 1934.

Cassius, Dio. *Roman History.* Translated by E. Carey, Loeb Classical Library, Vol. VII, 1924.

Danby, R. (trans.) *The Mishnah.* 1933.

Eusebius. *Ecclesiastical History.* Translated by K. Lake, Loeb Classical Library, 2 vols., 1926.

Josephus, F., *The Jewish War.*

——. *Jewish Antiquities.*

——. *Against Apion.*

——. *Life.*

Loeb Classical Library, 9 vols.

Slavonic Version, ed. by A. Berendts and K. Grass, 1926–27.

Pliny. *Natural History.*

Suetonius. *Lives of the Caesars.* ed. R. Graves, 1957.

——. *The Twelve Caesars.*

Tacitus. *Histories.* ed. J. Jackson, Loeb Classics, 1931–37.

——. *Annals.* 2nd ed. Translated by H. Furneuax, 1934.

Modern Works:

Abraham, I. *Campaigns in Palestine from Alexander the Great.* (Shweich Lectures, 1922), 1927.

Allegro, J. *The Dead Sea Scrolls.* 1956.

——. *The Treasure of the Copper Scroll.* 1960.

Angus, S. *The Religious Quests of the Graeco-Roman World.* 1929.

Arnold, W. T. *Roman Provincial Administration.* 1906.

Avi-Yonah, M. 'The Archaeological Survey of Masada,' *Israel Exploration Society Journal*, VII, 1957.
——. *The Third and Second Walls of Jerusalem*. Israel Exploration Society, 1968.
——. 'Map of Roman Palestine,' *Dept. of Antiquities of Palestine Quarterly*, V, 1936.
—— (with Y. Aharoni). *Bible Atlas*. 1968.
Baur, F. C. *Paul, His Life and Works*. 1845.
Bell, H. Idris. *Jews and Christians in Egypt*. 1924.
Bernstein, L. *Flavius Josephus, His Times and His Crisis*. 1938.
Brandon, S. G. F. *The Fall of Jerusalem and the Christian Church*. 1951.
——. *Jesus and the Zealots*. 1967.
——. *The Trial of Jesus*. 1968.
——. 'Josephus: Renegade or Patriot?' *History Today*, VIII, 1958.
——. 'The Defeat of Cestius Gallus, A.D. 66.' *History Today*, XX, 1970.
Buchler, A. *The Economic Condition of Judaea after the Destruction of the Second Temple*. 1912.
Charles R. M. *The Revelation of St John*. 2 vols. 1920.
Charlesworth, M. P. *Documents Illustrating the Reigns of Claudius and Nero*. 1939.
De Zuluetta, F. 'Violation of Sepulchre in Palestine at the Beginning of the Christian Era,' *Journal of Roman Studies*, XXII, 1932.
Dodd, C. H. 'The Fall of Jerusalem and the "Abomination of Desolation."' *Journal of Roman Studies*, XXXVIII, 1953–54.
Driver, G. R. *The Judaean Scrolls*. 1965.
Eisler, Robert. *The Messiah Jesus and John the Baptist*. 1931.
Farmer, W. R. *Maccabees, Zealots and Josephus*. 1956.
Foakes-Jackson, E. J. *Josephus and the Jews*. 1930.
Hart, H. S. J. 'Judaea and Rome: The Official Commentary,' *Journal of Theological Studies*, New Series III, 1952.
Hawkes, C. 'The Roman Siege of Masada,' *Antiquity*, III, 1929.
Hereford, R. T. *The Effect of the Fall of Jerusalem upon the Character of the Pharisees*, Soc. of Hebraic Studies, No. 2, 1917.

Hollis, F. J. *The Archaeology of Herod's Temple*. 1934.

Jeremais, J. *Jerusalem at the Time of Jesus*. 1969.

Jones, A. H. M. *The Herods of Judaea*. 1938.

Kennard, J. 'Judas of Galilee and His Clan,' *Jewish Quarterly Review*, XXXVI, 1945–46.

Kenyon, K. *Jerusalem: Excavating 3,000 Years of History*. 1967.

Klauser, R. *The Messianic Idea in Israel*. 1956.

——. *Jesus of Nazareth*. 1929.

Lewin, T. *The Siege of Jerusalem*. 1863.

Loewe, H. *'Render unto Caesar': Religious and Political Loyalty in Palestine*. 1940.

Marsden, E. W. *Greek and Roman Artillery*. 1969.

Moffat, James. *Introduction to the Literature of the New Testament*. 1928.

Momigliano, A. *L'Opera dell' Imperatore Claudios*. 1932.

——. *Josephus As a Source for the History of Judaea*. Cambridge Anc. Hist., 1934.

Mommsen, T. *Provinces of the Roman Empire*. 2 vols. 1886.

Montefiore, H. W. 'Sulpicius Severus and Titus' Council of War,' *Historia*, XI, 1962.

Morrison, W. D. *The Jews under Roman Rule*. 1890.

Mowinckel, S. *He That Cometh*. 1958.

Osterley, W. O. E. *History of Israel, Vol. II*. 1932.

Parker, H. M. D. *The Roman Legions*. 1958.

Richmond, J. A. 'The Roman Siege of Masada,' *Journal of Roman Studies*, LII, 1962.

Roth, C. 'The Constitution of the Jewish Republic, 66–70', *Journal of Semitic Studies*, IX, 1964.

——. 'The Zealots: A Jewish Religious Sect,' *Judaism*, VIII, 1959.

——. 'The Zealots in the War of 66–73,' *Journal of Semitic Studies*, IV, 1959.

——. 'The Debate on the Loyal Sacrifices A.D. 66,' *Harvard Theological Review*, LII, 1960.

——. 'The Pharisees in the Jewish Revolution of 66–73,' *Journal of Semitic Studies*, VII, 1962.

Schoeps, H. J. *Jewish Christianity*. 1969.

Schonfield, H. J. *History of Jewish Christianity*. 1936.

Schubertz, K. *Jewish Religious Parties and Sects : The Crucible of Christianity.* 1969.

Scramuzza, V. M. *The Policy of Early Roman Emperors towards Judaism.* (in Jackson and Lake. *Beginnings of Christianity, Vol. V*), 1933.

Shutt, R. J. H. *Studies in Josephus.* 1961.

Smallwood, E. M. 'Jews and Romans in the Early Empire,' *History Today*, XV. 1965.

Smith, J. A. *Jerusalem.* 2 vols. 1907.

Sukernik, E. L. (and L. A. Mayer). *The Third Wall of Jerusalem.* 1920.

Thackeray, H. StJ. *Josephus : The Man and the Historian.* 1929.

Toynbee, A. *Crucible of Christianity.* 1969.

Winter, P. *On the Trial of Jesus.* 1961.

Yadin, Y. *Masada : Herod's Fortress and the Zealots' Last Stand.* 1966.

Index

Index